WHAT READERS ARE SAYING...

"With the deconstruction of objective truth in today's postmodern culture, Glenn Henderson seeks to open the eyes of his readers to the reality of an ultimate truth. He reveals a truth that cannot be distorted or contaminated by the latest trends or the latest fads of any society. He reveals a truth that cannot be contained by anyone's relativism or a community's subjectivism.

"Glenn Henderson is a practitioner, and I have personally witnessed his truth uphold him and even define his purpose in a world that has lost its ability to reason. Awakened is what we all need to be at this hour. If you are serious about knowing if there is a right and wrong, good and evil, truth or no truth, open the pages of this book and then judge for yourselves. Who knows, the truth discovered by reading this book may become a lamp unto your feet and a guide for your pathway in life."

—Vaughn McLaughlin
CEO, Kingdom Plaza Mall

"Are you comfortable with what you believe? Do you feel you have a handle on today's social, political, moral, and ethical issues? If so, I suggest you avoid this book altogether. Honestly, it's not an easy read. It confronts issues few people want to think about, and it may even make you angry. Unlike other books of this nature, the author's goal is not agreement, but the willingness to look at the world through a different lens in order to validate whether what you believe is true or untrue. And let's face it, that's never easy or comfortable."

—Jim Chambers, EdD
Executive Leadership Coach and Trainer

Awaken

Breaking Free
From Societal Conformity to Unmask Truth

GLENN HENDERSON

GHEDI Press
Jacksonville, Florida

GHEDI Press
PO Box 50610
Jacksonville, FL 32240
www.GlennHenderson.com

979-8-9888839-2-0   print
979-8-9888839-3-7   ebook

Interior Design by Candace Ziegler
Cover Design by Bill Johnson

Publisher's Cataloging-in-Publication Data:
Names: Henderson, Glenn, 1958- author.
Title: Awaken : breaking free from societal conformity to unmask truth / Glenn Henderson.
Description: Jacksonville, FL : GHEDI Press, [2024] | Includes index.
Identifiers: ISBN: 979-8-9888839-2-0 (print) | 979-8-9888839-3-7 (ebook)
Subjects: LCSH: Awareness. | Conformity. | Truthfulness and falsehood. | Right and wrong. | Good and evil. | Social justice. | Social problems. | Christian life. | BISAC: SOCIAL SCIENCE / Sociology / General. | RELIGION / Christian Living / Social Issues.
Classification: LCC: BF311 .H46 2024 | DDC: 158.1--dc23

CONTENTS

INTRODUCTION

There is no debate that the world we now live in is ever-changing. Nothing seems stable.

Technology is progressing at lightning speed. There's talk of casual travel to space and populating planets such as Mars. New acronyms seem to crop up every day as people redefine themselves, refusing to stay within the confines of biology. Yet with all this *progress*, we're facing some of the highest suicide rates in recent history, alarming rises in Alzheimer's and autism diagnoses, and increasing crime and homelessness. It seems we are in a state of dis-ease.

Some would consider our world normal, others would say we are progressive, but some would argue that the culture is on a dangerous downward trend. They are worried about the path society is on but think they can't do anything to effect change.

We're often told that we can't think for ourselves, especially if we come to conclusions that do not align with popular opinion. So in these uncertain and unstable times, we're led to believe we can't comment on whether these changes are good or bad. We're also told everyone gets to determine what is good or bad based on personal experiences, beliefs, history, likes, and dislikes. The foam this churning has created is that change equals progress and evolution and, therefore, is innately good.

Going with the flow of the masses is popular, but I've had to ask myself, Is there a solution, a remedy, a place of stability amid all this confusion? In a world gone mad, is there any hope?

As a result, the following pages are a series of thoughts, ideas, and reflections about issues currently shaping our world, and therefore merit our attention. They are intended to stimulate your thinking, stir your heart, and challenge your preconceived ideas. The entries vary in length and intensity. Some are simple, some are complex, some are exciting, some are disturbing, but all are designed to confront our conventional thinking in hopes of unearthing the truth. In the end, I hope you will gain a deeper understanding of what is facing our world and be moved to action that would make the world a better place for us all.

I'm an optimist, a believer in the best. Even with all our differences, I trust that the greater majority of us want the same thing. But that same thing must have a basis if we are ever to attain it. The starting point is to be challenged by the idea of right and wrong, truth and falsehood, and not avoid the reality of good and evil.

Consider this: If we did not have evil, we would not know what good is. The opposition to the good helps teach us so we won't be duped by or become comfortable with lies trying to pass themselves off as truth.

Right and wrong are self-evident. For example, if you put your right foot into a left shoe, the shoe will not fit. Putting your right foot into a left shoe, or vice versa, is wrong, and walking with your shoes on the wrong feet will hurt. The longer you wear your shoes like that, the more discomfort you will experience. You can try to block out the pain, but it will persist until something changes. There is a right shoe and a wrong shoe for a person's foot, no matter how they feel, what others are saying, advances in technology, or discoveries in science.

There is a need for people to be *awakened* from their state of mind and from what the society is reflecting as acceptable. We can have different perspectives, but we must consider that some perspectives are skewed.

It is in this context that I address the concept of *truth*. Salt is a perfect metaphor for truth. Salt preserves and corrodes; it makes people so thirsty they will do anything to quench the dryness it creates. In large quantities, salt irritates, yet when the proper quantity is applied in the proper place, it can be a healing agent.

Salt adds flavor, but too much makes food unpalatable and even harmful to the body. Salt does many things and is used for multiple purposes. It is loved when it serves us well, and disliked—even hated—when its effect is adverse. However, when all is said and done, salt is simply salt. The same holds true of truth. Regardless of its impact—whether it's loved or hated, provokes joy or irritation—truth cannot be denied.

We feel the value of salt most when it is missing. Ancient wisdom says, "If the salt loses its saltiness…it is no longer good for anything, except to be thrown out and trampled underfoot."[1] Those who negate truth are the ones trampling on it.

Often we seek to avoid or deny that which cannot be denied. Ultimately, though, we all will come face to face with truth. We must think of truth as salt. You don't have to like it; salt may irritate and cause erosion, but its absence will be felt. Regardless of all opinions, truth, if absent, renders things tasteless and all positions and pseudo progress good for nothing.

This book considers the many truths we need to be awakened to. We must, at a minimum, agree that the right foot belongs in the right shoe and the left foot should be in the left shoe.

My aim in writing this book is to help us rediscover what is true. I did not write it to convince or change anyone. Rather, I offer it to consider that it's possible for any of us to be misguided. We all can be wrong, but we all cannot be right! Each entry is intended to provoke the reader to determine if what they've just read is wrong. The next question is, How is it wrong? Is the problem found in what was portrayed, how it was presented, the outcome, or some combination of those three?

Again, agreement is not the goal. Not only is it almost impossible that everyone agree (as it should be); it is also not a solution because we can all agree and all be wrong! I am not looking for agreement, but I invite you to judge whether what is presented is right or wrong, true or false.

When I think about the current state of the world—where we are, where we were, and the transitions in our society—I realize that the loudest voices are often those promoting, supporting, or advancing the conditions that led us where we are. Are the voices shaping our culture actually telling us right, or are they just loud?

As we hear and embrace what is being promoted in society, are we putting our right foot in the left shoe? The old adage says, if the shoe fits, wear it. But the converse is also true: if the shoe doesn't fit, leave it at the store. All too often, we do not agree that our shoe does not fit. We force our feet into them anyway, and over time we become so familiar with the pain that it no longer bothers us, or we just become willing to live with it. But we know something is wrong; we know the wrong foot is in the shoe.

The entries in this book are presented in agreement but not for agreement. This is to say, each entry reflects someone's position or experience. And some have scientific support, though science continues to learn and change.

The objective of these entries is to present facts and truth. The difference between those concepts is subtle but significant. Facts prove (support, reflect) a person's position, beliefs, and even status, and they change with the person's position, beliefs, and status. Truth, however, is not impacted by facts. It precedes and stands after the facts. Truth is not biased. It doesn't care about public opinion. It's willing to take on all challengers. But its greatest attribute may be that it stands the test of time. It never changes or evolves and is devoid of opinion or feelings. It cannot be schooled and always proves itself to be truth.

Change for the sake of change is not progress. My hope is that as you engage each entry, you will consider the perspective being offered and let it motivate you to seek the truth and refuse to let it be suppressed.

Section 1

WORLDVIEW

The Importance of Worldview

THE WORLD AROUND us is shaped by the world within us, so how we see that world is important to our present and future success.

Someone has said that the eye is the lamp of the body, which simply means that the lens through which we view life will determine our thoughts, actions, experiences, and ultimately our destiny.

In this section, I challenge you to clarify what you believe in order to distinguish it from other views.

1

SUCCESS

B EWARE OF SUCCESS, for when success is achieved, there will always be a demanding responsibility adjoined to it! Always!

The idea of success is a big part of American culture, as well as other cultures around the world. How we define success may differ, but the idea that with success comes increased responsibility is widely accepted.

Someone once said "with much power comes much responsibility," or to put it another way, "To him who has much, much is expected, required and even demanded."

When you are successful in your field, the spotlight is on you, and there is an expectation that you will do something productive or useful with the power and resources you now have at your disposal. There is an expectation of contribution for the benefit of others, and often society as a whole. It doesn't matter if you are in the public eye or remain obscure; you are expected to do something positive with what you now have, whether it is money, power, influence, notoriety, or any other resources.

Therefore, the question is, If you reach your goal of being successful, are you ready to accept the responsibility that comes along with it?

2

EIGHT POSSIBILITIES OF BELIEF

B ECAUSE MONEY IS two-faced, what we believe about it, and how we arrive at that conclusion, is essential to how we leverage it. Here are eight possibilities of belief about money.

1. We believe what we choose to believe.

2. We believe what we are told to believe.

3. We believe what the masses believe.

4. We believe what is presented (in the news or social media).

5. We believe what works. (If it works, it must be right! Right?)

6. We believe in what suits us, our philosophy.

7. We believe in what feels good.

8. We believe only what can be verified as true.

Because many of these statements are incompatible with one another, we can't believe they are all true. As a result, we are forced to choose which one we believe is true, and more importantly, which one is going to guide our thoughts and decisions about money.

One way to determine where we are in our current belief system is by using the process of elimination. By systematically eliminating all the statements we believe are untrue about our situation right now, we can narrow it down to what we believe is most true as we go forward.

——————— 3 ———————

GET RID OF YOUR BAGGAGE

T HERE WAS MORE baggage in my storage unit than I realized," a colleague confessed, so I listened as he told the following story.

While at my storage unit recently, I saw a large group of Hispanic people congregating by their cars in the parking lot as others from the group were at a nearby food truck. For some reason, I felt uneasy and asked myself, "Why am I feeling unsettled? Why would a dark-skinned man, a minority, feel uneasy around another group of minorities? Where did this baggage come from?"

It's usually me who makes others feel uneasy, and yet the tables had been turned, and I was feeling different and apprehensive.

The group was simply minding their own business and enjoying themselves, and yet I wondered, "Have I been conditioned to fear them because of the media's portrayal? Have I been taught to see people in a particular way through the images constantly portrayed by media outlets? Why am I feeling so uneasy?"

I had to fight against my common sense and experience as a minority. I know firsthand what it is like to be judged by people who form the kinds of misguided, misinformed conclusions I was making at that moment. I was struggling to resist the notion planted in my mind by society that everyone in a particular group is the same. I had come to think of this community of people as poor, up to no good, and at worst, filled with drug dealers. Knowing firsthand how I am perceived as a minority, I asked myself, "How did this baggage get here? What made me think a certain way and then become so uneasy?"

Many groups of people around the globe have been portrayed as being on the lower rungs of society's totem pole. Native Americans, Hispanics, and Africans are just a few of the groups viewed as having a lower skill set. They have been taken advantage of, paid lower wages, and offered fewer opportunities than traditional Western Europeans. Minorities are often characterized as willing to do work others do not want to do, so they are portrayed as inferior or less than others.

This baggage I know firsthand.

Sometimes, they are allowed, or forced, to work under the table and then labeled as illegal aliens. Regardless of the nametag, their treatment is the most telling and so what helped inform my thoughts and feelings about the people I was encountering at the moment.

This group of people would work on weekends and holidays, in good weather or bad, without complaining. Even if they did complain, I would not fully understand what they were saying because of the language barrier. However, I also didn't care about their complaints because I knew many of the jobs they were offered here were an upgrade from jobs in their home country. Now, as a result of this experience, I was beginning to question the origins of my own thinking.

As I considered the cause of my uneasiness, I recalled the media images of people crossing the US border illegally. I remembered news reports of walls being built to keep them from coming into the nation. I recalled the images of people who, thinking they were escaping oppression, discrimination, and a lack of opportunity, fled to a land of freedom and opportunity.

So many images crossed my mind—of people willing to risk their lives by using any mode of transportation regardless of condition to reach the land of opportunity. I saw images of cars, vans, boats, and trailers without windows or proper ventilation packed with people. I saw their faces more than the mode of transportation. This was when I began to see there was more baggage in my emotional and mental storage unit than I realized.

The way minorities are portrayed by the media contains an element of truth that is often good; it depicts uniqueness, difference, and cultural diversity. While those distinctions should be appreciated and celebrated, they are often represented by the media in the worst manner. Their differences are used to make minorities appear of less value, and because of this, I had to fight the temptation to have a negative image of the Hispanics across the parking lot from me.

In addition, the baggage I saw as I looked at them was a reflection of what had been portrayed in the media but not necessarily what I had personally experienced. In addition, the baggage wasn't just something stuffed away in storage until needed; I was carrying it around.

As I got out of my BMW, I realized the mixed and unsettling feeling was that I had been influenced to think these people wanted to harm me and were up to no good. I immediately got in touch with my emotions and recognized what unsettled me. Then I noticed another piece of baggage I now think of as luggage.

I discovered that my concern about this group of people was directly related to my status in life. I immediately considered that I was driving my luxury car, and from what I could see, they weren't driving luxury vehicles.

Then I began to think, "I wonder what they are thinking as they see me and my car."

This contributed to my uneasiness. What if they thought I was among those who oppressed and took advantage of them? Or perhaps they thought that despite being viewed as cheap labor, receiving lesser jobs, and never being made to feel equal, they should be grateful for what they had. Surely I know how it feels to be mistreated and lumped into a group by uninformed observers who think that everyone in an ethnic group believes, thinks, and acts the same way.

"Why am I carrying these thoughts around with me?" I asked myself. Even as someone discriminated against, I had to work to dismiss the idea that being a minority equates to being up to no good. I was fighting off what my mind told me about them: "You must protect yourself from them. You know what they think as they see you." I continued to hear from my baggage, which now had become my luggage.

Despite these thoughts, I locked my doors and kept an eye on all their moves, ensuring I was safe from them. As I reflect on the situation, it is almost funny when I consider that none of them even paid attention to me, as far as I could tell. They were minding their own business and having fun while I was uneasy and unsettled.

After I was safely locked in my car, I thought, "Suppose some of them were paying attention to me, plotting something?" I had something they didn't have. And I knew in my heart, this proposition was the foundation of my uneasiness. I'd found the source of my baggage.

My mind raced through the images of how "they" are treated. Even with no personal experiences to support the notion that "they" are dangerous, I began to imagine that they could have acted exactly as portrayed. My uneasiness resulted from anticipating what had been planted in my mind. It was baggage weighing me down and luggage I was carrying around!

"If they did something to me, would I or anyone have been surprised?" I wondered. I then recalled a statement that stuck with me: "We create our own demons." It applied so clearly to my baggage, which was now my luggage.

This was indeed a conundrum. I struggled with two realities. First, as a minority, I knew how this felt. Second, I had been made to feel a certain way by people who don't know how it feels to be a minority.

I began conversing with myself, naming things that should never happen. People should never be lumped into one category simply because they are categorized as a minority. An entire group should never be judged as needy based on appearances. And they should never—no, never—be judged based on the way they have been portrayed or treated. All people can't act as they are represented in the media.

After further self-examination, I realized my fears (baggage) were made up of several layers.

The first and most apparent layer was from views created by outside sources, real or imagined, that affected how I see people. Under the sun, image is everything. It has been said that man looks on the outside, but God looks at the heart. I was focused on the outside, not thinking of what kind of people they might be: loving, kind-hearted, etc.

The second layer was my perception beyond the first look—not what I see but how I perceive and categorize what I see. The human condition is interesting. We see people as less than or more than based on the luggage we carry around. My mental and emotional image of them was less than admirable, and I had to come to grips with my own false perception.

None of this resolved my fears and uneasiness until I realized that, first, we should see people as equals, neither less than nor more than ourselves. If a person looks successful, is neatly dressed, and is well-groomed, we typically think we have little or nothing to fear. We often draw this conclusion with little regard for skin color. We are more ready to accept, let our guard down, and engage with those who look a certain way.

If people look like they have things (a group I call the "*haves*"), others tend to drop their guard almost entirely. Having similar possessions and lifestyles, the *haves* are fearless among themselves, but they fear being around the *have-nots*. This was apparently at the core of my baggage.

The *haves* are a unified family glued together by success, money, and earned or inherited privilege. I saw this more clearly as I discovered more luggage than baggage—what I was carrying around versus what weighed me down.

In considering all this, I realized another truth: the *haves* are fearful of the *have-nots*, and the *have-nots* are just as afraid of the *haves*. We fear one another for similar but different reasons.

The *haves* fear the *have-nots* for what they have done to them, real or contrived, and the *have-nots* fear the *haves* for the same reason. The glaring difference is that the *have-nots* usually want to get to know the *haves*, but there is a sense of fear. They are afraid to approach and wonder what the *haves* will say or do. They think, "Perhaps I won't be well-received" because of their lack of riches, status, or other social standing.

The *haves* don't want to get to know the *have-nots*. But even in that, there is fear. The *haves* are almost always afraid to approach the *have-nots* for a variety of reasons.

I wondered, "Who has more baggage, the *haves* or the *have-nots*?" It was becoming clear to me that the *haves* have more baggage (issues), but the *have-nots'* baggage is heavier to bear in the long run. Both carry their luggage, but the *haves* carry their luggage out of desire, and the *have-nots* do so because it is an imposed burden and often impossible to escape.

I considered the source of the fears that might exist between the two. The *have-nots'* heavier baggage is from the high probability that they will be ridiculed, humiliated, belittled, patronized, ignored, and feared. It is not because of what they have and what they can do but because of what they don't have and cannot do. Perception comes first and reality second. They are treated like and made to be the *haves'* luggage.

We all carry luggage; we all have baggage. Try lightening the load. Try carrying one another's luggage and get rid of everyone's baggage.

$$*\ *\ *\ *\ *$$

Some people would call his experience nonsense. But after hearing my colleague's experience, I thought, "He has been *awakened*!"

4

SENSE MEETS "KNOW SENSE"

EVERYONE TRIES TO make sense of the world. However, a wise man once said, "Gold there is, and rubies in abundance, but lips that speak knowledge are a rare jewel."[1] Sense is good, but what is better is to add wisdom and knowledge—to "know" sense.

ONE WORLD TWO VIEWS

Sense: There is no need for a plumb line. Who are you to tell me what to do or not to do, what is right or wrong? If there is a plumb line, I will establish mine, and you can establish yours. Sometimes we say, "To each his own. Live and let live."

Know Sense: If everyone establishes his or her own plumb line, there is no plumb line.

Sense: We all should be able to determine what's right and wrong on our own and not be told what is good or bad, as each of us has our own experiences and can learn from them and even teach others.

Know Sense: The problem is that each of us interprets our experiences differently and will put a stake in the ground and say with the greatest conviction, "I am right." Nevertheless, is it possible for more than one person, or countless people, with varying positions on the same matter to all be right?

Sense: OK, perhaps you have a small point on the plumb line. But that still does not negate my privilege or right to determine what is right or wrong for me.

Know Sense: There is a right and wrong, regardless of what you think, say, or believe. In fact, you will say this very statement is either right or wrong.

Sense: I may consider that there is a right and wrong outside my opinion. However, good and evil—who are you to determine what is good or evil? You have gone too far!

Know Sense: The conditions you have been and are now experiencing directly result from ignoring the plumb line, thus removing it from its intended, foundational purpose. This has resulted in good being called evil and evil being called good. As Isaiah 5:20 says, "Woe to those who call evil good and good evil, who put darkness for light and light for darkness, who put bitter for sweet and sweet for bitter."

Sense: Even if I remotely believe this, is there any way out of this mess or dilemma?

Know Sense: Yes, a way has been provided, but the way originally offered has been denied. The denial has become a trap, tricking you into accepting an alternative, self-serving way. The trap and the way are spoken of in Genesis 3:22: "And the LORD God said, 'The man has now become like one of us, knowing good and evil. He must not be allowed to reach out his hand and take also from the tree of life and eat, and live forever.'"

Sense: How can knowing good and evil be a trap? Assuming I may believe in God, what would be wrong with wanting to be like God?

Know Sense: Humans knowing good and evil is very different from knowing the *difference* between good and evil. When humans try to be like God, there is going to be a problem. Trying to be like God—something you can never attain—while knowing good and evil is how you've ended up in your current condition in the first place.

Sense: With our knowledge, humans have achieved and excelled and can boast many advances. As a society, we have accomplished much that cannot be argued. We have ventured to the depths of the seas and soared to the stars in the sky. We have cured many diseases. We have engineered the impossible in buildings, cities, and bridges; our achievements are incredible.

Know Sense: You can have knowledge without having wisdom. Being aware of something is just that—being aware. It can be tied to knowledge, but there is a difference between having knowledge of something and knowing something or someone. Your advancements are based upon your knowledge and understanding. But look around you. Is the world a better place? Don't assess that based on your opinion or the result of your efforts. Look at the people around you and ask them how society has changed due to human knowledge. Don't ask the people in your high-rises but those you pass on the way to the high rises.

Sense: I know what I know, and what you say makes *no sense* to me. What are you saying?

Know Sense: It was said that Adam knew his wife and she conceived a child.[2] The scripture indicates that Adam connected physically with his wife—he *knew* Eve. Adam didn't just have knowledge of her; he had emotional, physical, and spiritual intimacy with her. When you have true knowledge that gives understanding, what you know then leads to life through the application of knowledge and wisdom, which is the best use of knowledge. If it kills or stifles life, it is not the intended purpose of knowledge and almost always lacks wisdom.

Sense: No sense, nonsense; I don't "know" how to make sense of this. Please explain.

Know Sense: Cancer kills life. Anything that kills or destroys life is anti-life. Cancer destroys and ends. Eliminating or killing cancer eliminates that which kills life so life can continue.

Sense: Oh, sure, that makes perfect sense …

Know Sense: It makes perfect sense to you, yet humans continue to violate this principle and even pass laws contrary to good sense. You have created and passed laws that destroy life while advancing others that do not promote life!

Sense: Most of us are doing our best and using our knowledge as we learn, grow, and evolve.

Know Sense: By now, you should know you do not have the knowledge or possess what is necessary in and of yourself. Frankly, you cannot in and of yourself make the best decisions based on your knowledge. This has been proven throughout history. Medicine continues to be a practice. Science continues to evolve. Professors continue to profess that there is a problem as they defend their plumb line and are met with the same convictions from their colleagues. Pundits, purists, and professionals argue and debate among themselves in the name of higher learning, seeking the truth, and arriving at utopia. But they agree on one thing: that there is no plumb line, right or wrong, good or evil, light or darkness.

Sense: The professors and learned arguing among themselves are misguided and thus wrong in what they do. They should agree with one another.

Know Sense: You just said they are "wrong in what they do." This affirms that there is a right and wrong. Now we see the need for a plumb line that exists outside all of us. What makes one position superior to another? All are the same if all use the same thing and follow the same rules. "Know sense"—knowledge and wisdom—is the basis of a plumb line. When something is wrong, the outcome of knowledge regarding that matter is tested by wisdom. It is with that knowledge the necessary plumb line is revealed.

Sense: Are you saying that the only way I can find myself at a place of rest, advancement, or progress is for us to establish a place of agreement that is not dependent on any individual or experience? Moreover, must it be based on the truth that, though challenged or even ignored, stands the test of time as it proves itself?

Know Sense: Alas, we arrive at an epiphany that there must be an established, unchangeable standard that we all agree on and that is never to change (i.e., a plumb line). Can men and women agree on a standard that will and should never change, as it is the plumb line to be used for generations to come? Though attacked or challenged, the standard should remain unchanged because it is the plumb line, even if it is said to be outdated and obsolete in different times and circumstances.

Sense: OK, let's assume I agree. Who is worthy of establishing the plumb line? I'm willing to establish the plumb line, the standard. Why not me?

Know Sense: We must realize that none of us can establish the plumb line. Something defective cannot make something without defect. The imperfect cannot make something perfect. We must together seek to discover the plumb line and realize that it does not adjust to us; we must adjust to it.

Sense: If not me or you, then who establishes the standard for what makes sense?

Know Sense: All humans have their own agendas, which are innately deficient and bring their own problems. We have choice, creativity, and ability, but we are still deficient. We are made in God's image, but we are not God. The serpent told Eve, "For God knows that when you eat from [the tree of the knowledge of good and evil] your eyes will be opened, and you will be like God, knowing good and evil."[3] The serpent's words were misleading, though enticing. The finite creation can never surpass or even match the infinite Creator in understanding, wisdom, or sovereignty.

Sense: If I am going along with the "know sense" idea, which is still nonsense to me and in some moments makes no sense, what shall I do to continue?

Know Sense: There is a right and wrong, and what is right and wrong, good and evil is based on a plumb line, set not by the defective but the perfect. In addition, this plumb line gives hope. Genesis 4:7 says, "If you do what is right, will you not be accepted?"

Sense: Nonsense. This makes no sense. What do you mean by "know sense"?

Know Sense: You cannot truly know right from wrong, good from evil by relying on that which was created by your own hands. We tend to cover the truth and see a lie.

Sense: What can possibly be wrong—assuming, just for conversation, there is a wrong—with covering something when it needs to be covered?

Know Sense: Relying on your created plumb line, the things you must have to guide and cover you will leave you feeling naked and afraid. You cannot cover your nakedness your way, as Genesis 3:7 tells us Adam and Eve tried to do. After they ate of the fruit, "Then the eyes of both of them were opened, and they realized they were naked; so they sewed fig leaves together and made coverings for themselves."

Sense: I'm still not feeling this, and I am certainly against being converted into believing there is a right or wrong absent of my choosing—a good or evil that I cannot define. What am I missing?

Know Sense: The right clothes must be made for you, and you must wear them. We cannot make the right clothes for ourselves. Hard as we may try, we cannot establish our own right and wrong or good or evil plumb line. Genesis 3:21–24 says: "The LORD God made garments of skin for Adam and his wife and clothed them. And the LORD God said, 'The man has now become like one of us, knowing good and evil. He must not be allowed to reach out his hand and take also from the tree of life and eat, and live forever.' So the LORD God banished him from the Garden of Eden to work the ground from which he had been taken. After he drove the man out, he placed on the east side of the Garden of Eden cherubim and a flaming sword flashing back and forth to guard the way to the tree of life."

Sense: OK, so I cannot go back, even though this still makes no sense to me and is sometimes even nonsense. However, I cannot argue or deny reality and how I feel. The times are scary, and I am very much afraid. Now, Know Sense, tell me something …

Know Sense: You now know what you are feeling, sensing, and experiencing, but you don't know why. When things begin to unravel, truth, a plumb line, still stands, and when having to face reality, one becomes afraid. Genesis 3:10 says, "[Adam] answered, 'I heard you in the garden, and I was afraid because I was naked; so I hid.'"

Sense: I did not realize that my feelings and experiences resulted from being naked. I don't feel naked. I have clothing, protection, and a place to live. I must admit, though, I do ask, Why am I uneasy and fearful? With your "know sense" explanation, I am considering that I might be naked.

Know Sense: Your nakedness was fine with Me; it was even OK with you until you had your eyes opened through your own actions under your own will. When you try and be "like" Me, you come to know and even experience good and evil. All things were good when the focus was on Me or something outside of you. It was just like Genesis 2:25, which says Adam and his wife were both naked, and they felt no shame.

Sense: If I am to believe any of this, I must understand what happened.

Know Sense: Adam and Eve were simply enjoying what was intended—unashamed nakedness, purity, and vulnerability. They didn't need to hide or be guarded, as the innocence that accompanies divine design was already in place. It was only after a selfish, self-serving choice was made that it became clear how errant that choice was. When the focus is on self, nakedness is revealed. Having removed yourself from being divinely covered, you must once again be covered, as you have been exposed as naked and removed from your intended design. You had been given a covering that fits so well you didn't even know you were naked. Though naked, you were never exposed because you had been divinely covered.

They became exposed as they exchanged the Creator's plumb line (His standards of rule) for the creation's plumb line (man's standard of rule).

Sense: Yeah, OK, that explains nothing other than at times I realized something was not right. I didn't really know what was wrong, yet I took action. For that at least, we mere mortals should be applauded, and it should be acknowledged that we do know some things!

Know Sense: Indeed, you now know some things but not all or even the right things. Again, taking matters into your own hands and trying to cover your nakedness by your own effort will prove to be unfruitful. Genesis 3:7 says, "Then the eyes of both of them were opened, and they realized they were naked; so they sewed fig leaves together and made coverings for themselves." Practically speaking, leaves cannot adequately cover anyone. Animal skin is better, but it also falls short.

Sense: Then what is the best covering so I can stop running, hiding, and being afraid?

Know Sense: "The Lord God made garments of skin for Adam and his wife and clothed them."[4] Doing things in your own strength will prove to be only a temporary and ineffective solution at best. You have proven this yourself. Thus, it is necessary to make some sense of things. It is time to know wisdom and knowledge. It is time you "know sense."

Sense: Well, OK, but suppose I do not want someone else to cover me? In addition, though I know things are dicey, I am still not convinced I am naked. I think I will just go about my business.

Know Sense: Knowledge of the Creator differs from the knowledge of humans trying to be like the Creator. Those who look to provide their own covering are those who are most in need of it.

Sense: I know what I know, and no one tells me what I know or do not know.

Know Sense: I get it. Go about your business. You are covered by your own hands, accomplishments, and achievements. Nevertheless, you do not realize yet that the covering you have made is temporary and as inadequate as fig leaves. Even human sacrifices fall short in covering nakedness. This is why you are still not at peace, even with all you have accomplished, acquired, and achieved. You continue to look for ways to protect what you have gained. You sleep peacefully only when you have kept others away or down. Only then are you joyful and somewhat at rest, as there is always something to protect, something to keep others from getting. And alas, you find rest when relaxing in protected, gated places, away from those who threaten all you worked for and feel entitled to enjoy. You have covered yourself. However, remember, when you take a cover from one place, it uncovers another. "You say, 'I am rich; I have acquired wealth and do not need a thing.' But you do not realize that you are wretched, pitiful, poor, blind and naked."[5]

Sense: You have offended me, and after thinking these things through further, I disagree with everything you have said. I do not agree with you and your "know sense," which, in fact, is nonsense and makes no sense. I am not naked, and I am not ashamed as you say I am. Be gone with this nonsense, which makes no sense.

Know Sense: You have spoken correctly, and that is the problem. You are not unashamed, as you do not admit to your nakedness, though it is right before you. Until you can be naked and unashamed—free from running, looking back, locking doors, worrying about tomorrow, wondering when enough is enough—you will continue to run, work more, sleep less, and wake up to a world that you cannot identify with. You will continue on this path until you are in right standing with God, having nothing to hide or be ashamed of as a result Him clothing you. This can only happen when you come clean, admitting your nakedness—your exposure—and that you've been relying on yourself.

Sense: My nakedness and exposure are a result of doing my own thing and depending on self rather than truth?

Know Sense: It is as you say—you now *know sense*.

KNOWLEDGE

We Don't Know What We Don't Know

THE LONGER WE are alive, the more we know about ourselves, others, and the world around us. We also don't know what we don't know.

The ancients believed that a time would come when knowledge would surpass wisdom, and given the current state of the world, we may be closer to that time than we think. Knowing something doesn't mean we always use the information wisely, and so knowledge alone can become dangerous very quickly.

In this section, we will look at what it means to be knowledgeable and at the same time have the wisdom necessary to use it wisely.

— 5 —

DESPISE NOT

THE *HAVE-NOTS*—THOSE WHO have not attained, those oppressed, those waiting for their chance, those the system and life have dealt a bad hand—must resist despising the people who have (the people they aspire to be) or hate the things they have yet to attain. Despising and hating others could be why they do not achieve what they desire. Despising others holds the person who hates in captivity, preventing them from being blessed.

One of our human weaknesses is the dislike we feel for what we cannot attain, or that society cannot provide.

Many people (the *have-nots*) dream of becoming millionaires, but when they realize it is unlikely, they look on millionaires (the *haves*) with distain, suspicion, or jealousy.

The opposite can also be true when a *have-not* becomes successful. The very people they disliked because of their money, power, and influence, they now value because they are part of the same group. We must caution ourselves in how we view others, as it is possible that our view of others may be the very thing that keeps us from excelling.

So, how do you feel about the *haves* of the world? Do you appreciate what they have accomplished, or are they viewed as suspect? If you achieved their status, becoming a *have*, how would you feel about your prior feelings toward those who have?

— 6 —

THE SPOTLIGHT—BELIEVE IN IT

SOCIETY SAYS, "WE will *make* you believe in yourself, and afterward, we will *break* you from believing in yourself."

Individuals in the spotlight of the public eye often learn how quickly the tide can turn against them.

For example, one minute you are the darling of Wall Street, and the next you are sitting in jail awaiting trial. Politics is another example. One minute you are in a position of power and authority, and the next you are on the nightly news defending yourself against accusations of wrongdoing. The same is true for entertainers and sports figures, who are celebrated by the media on a grand scale, and then find themselves no longer loved.

Public success is a slippery slope, and the truth is, we set people up for failure by making them superstars in the first place. Then we stand by with a critical eye as they fall out of favor at the hands of those who put them in the spotlight.

— 7 —

DESTINY

IF YOU BUY a commodity early on and engage in things connected to it as an owner, you can significantly influence its future. However, the outcome is largely shaped by the masses and investors who take an interest in the activity of the commodity. They shape how it is perceived. If the commodity, especially a human commodity such as a sports figure, is self-aware, it would also have influence over how it perceives itself and exert additional influence on the outcome.

While the owner may influence the commodity, the masses have a greater role in shaping it, and other forces can manipulate it. Considering all this, there is no way to guarantee how everything will ultimately turn out.

We can know that if the commodity does not perform well—if it doesn't meet expectations or survive public scrutiny—it can be sold, traded, or eliminated from ownership. If the commodity were self-aware and realized it was not wanted or had lost its value, glory, and luster, it could remove itself from the market.

We say people are free and they alone determine their destiny, but are they? We say we make our own choices, but we don't always want to admit that like commodities, outside forces can influence our destiny.

--------- 8 ---------

THERE IS NOTHING TO LOSE

THE PEOPLE WHO are the most fearful of others having what they possess are those who think they have something to lose. They are guarded, living in fear without knowing why they are afraid. Fear is typically believed to be just a feeling. However, in this case, it is more of a sickness, as fear is connected to loss. As a result of possible or pending loss, fear sets in.

The antidote to this sickness is to realize you own nothing and, therefore, have nothing to lose. This is how to diminish fear of loss.

Since the beginning of time, every person arrives in this world with nothing and relies on things being given to them. It is hoped and expected that they will work to gain temporal possessions. However, no one arrives with anything, and despite all that we can accomplish, we depart with nothing as well.

Of course, some have the things they attained while on earth buried with their lifeless bodies. They have taken these material things to their grave or their final, earthly resting place, but they have not taken those items with them into the afterlife.

After a time, their physical bodies will decay, and only their skeletons will remain. However, the things they owned will be left behind. This is true without exception.

No matter how hard you try, when it is your time to die, there is little you can do or say to influence the timing of your passing. The reality is that you have no control over your exit. Life is brief, death is often sudden, and all you gain will be left behind. Therefore, you truly have nothing to lose when your mindset as you go through life is to manage possessions instead of thinking you own them. If you live as a manager instead of an owner, you will have nothing to lose in every case.

Free yourself from the fruitless effort of trying to protect what is not yours. If it ever is yours, whether earned or given, it is only for a short time—while you still have breath. In every case, this proves you have nothing to lose, because you didn't own it in the first place.

It is possible to die having lived a life fearlessly. You can truly be free from fear of loss when you realize you have nothing to lose.

There is an exception, however. It was once said, "What would it profit a person to gain the whole world and lose their soul?"[1]

Therefore, it seems you do have something to lose by living a fearless life, understanding that what you gain in possessions is temporary.

9

THE RULES OF ECONOMICS, PART 1

I N THE 1960s, there was a sci-fi TV series called *The Outer Limits*. It was a production ahead of its time, evident from its opening. Most would agree the concept was clever and compelling, even if it seemed preposterous and ridiculous at the time.

Each week, the show opened with these words: "There is nothing wrong with your television set. Do not attempt to adjust the picture. We are controlling transmission. We will control the horizontal. We will control the vertical. We can change the focus to a soft blur or sharpen it to crystal clarity. For the next hour, sit quietly, and we will control all that you see and hear. You are about to participate in a great adventure. You are about to experience the awe and mystery which reaches from the inner mind to…the outer limits!"[1]

The opening describes much of what we are living, experiencing, and witnessing: the outer limits of our world!

Is calling it a conspiracy harsh? Perhaps not, but ignorance and being uninformed, unaware, and even in denial are convenient outs to the unfathomable notion of being under the influence or control of others. The idea of being controlled is shocking to our humanity, and we would immediately reject and resist if we suspected someone of trying to control us.

We loathe the thought of being controlled or, better said, of being subjected to unwanted influences because we naturally oppose the idea of being manipulated.

One of the easiest and most effective ways to exert control over someone is to do so when the person enjoys what is happening to them and does not realize what is truly going on. As the news can no longer be trusted, though it is in abundance through many distribution channels, its effectiveness and value have been minimized. Mainstream news has lost its dominance, and entertainment is now used to control. The thinking is, "If you can get the people to enjoy what we are looking to do, there will be little to no resistance; even better, they will look forward to it. They will even 'pay' for it!"

"They will even pay for it" is ironic intentionally! Perhaps the greatest example of using entertainment to exert control over people is through sports. Sports are enjoyed in every region globally, from the smallest to the largest and everything in between. Sports are one of the most popular categories of television programming.

Sports are woven into the fabric of our society, perhaps out of need or desire to compete or vicariously experience a different reality. Unlike other forms of entertainment, a sport sets itself apart, as it touches virtually every human emotion. Sports are the universal language, following just one step behind money.

Sports command global attention. The Olympics is, perhaps, the most significant sports event in that it boasts bringing people from around the world to one stage. Other sports are international too. Soccer and golf have competitors from numerous nations, and the countries compete against one another.

In the United States, baseball has the World Series, but the competition is not between countries. Football is the most popular sport in the United States, and its championship game is called the Super Bowl. There are developed and undeveloped countries that are significantly larger than the United States, not only geographically but also in terms of population. Yet more attention is given to US sports than all others. The United States has the most prolific, prodigious distribution network in terms of technology and marketing dollars to fuel this form of entertainment and its greatest asset, the athletes.

Other countries have platforms, but the broadcasts of their sports are censored within those nations. In some cases, broadcasts from the United States are not allowed to be aired in those countries. However, the United States stands first in the production of diverse sports content.

We must remember that while sports are a competition and players consider it their job, the casual viewer sees sports as entertainment. It is a significant factor in our world. Sports games are played by professionals whose job is to play the game, and the masses gamble on the results. Television networks promote the competition as entertainment, the best-known being ESPN, the Entertainment and Sports Programming Network.

Given that sports is entertainment, the broadcasters whose voices we hear are characterized as hosts. Facts are blended with opinions to reflect what they want you to see and hear as the athletes entertain you.

Some entertainment executives might say: "There is no need for accountability or journalistic responsibility among sportscasters, and if there ever is such a need, we reserve the right to do as we see fit because sports is entertainment. We control the assets—what you see and hear! We control the assets behind the microphones, in front of the cameras, and on the field. We will tell you what to like and dislike. We will tell you when it is good that someone has come out of the closet and when it would be best for them to go into the closet."

We flock to the multitude of streaming services and are mesmerized, almost hypnotized, because we enjoy what we see. It is entertainment to us but control to them. "We control. We will take you on a journey." What was once just a ridiculous, perhaps preposterous, opening to a TV show is now a reality.

This is the rule of economics: "They" control the outer limits of the assets!

10

THE RULES OF ECONOMICS, PART 2

THERE IS NOTHING wrong with your television set. Do not attempt to adjust the picture. We are controlling transmission. We will control the horizontal. We will control the vertical. We can change the focus to a soft blur or sharpen it to crystal clarity. For the next hour sit quietly, and we will control all that you see and hear. You are *experiencing* a great adventure. You *are experiencing* the awe and mystery that reaches from the inner mind to...the outer limits!"[1]

Those last two sentences have been altered slightly from the opening lines of the 1960s TV show *The Outer Limits* to reflect our reality.

The depth and reach of control in the world of sports, which we enjoy as entertainment, is beyond the assets. When economics is applied strategically to the geographic of sports, access can be controlled.

In the world of sports, perhaps more than in any other profession, geography directly contributes to and shapes the sport itself. Consider that athletes who play hockey, ski, or snowboard often come from colder climates. Those athletes also happen to be, by and large, white in terms of their skin color. Most of our world-class runners come from warmer climates and are darker in terms of their skin color.

Swimming, being an indoor sport, is primarily popular among those who have a white skin color. Basketball, although more international now, is still primarily played by those with dark skin color. Football is interesting, since most of the players have a dark skin color, but the number of coaches, quarterbacks, and team owners with a dark skin color is in single digits. The sport played most universally in America, regardless of age or ethnicity, is controlled like no other by those whose skin color is white. This is not a criticism, just a fact.

While each sport is distinct, there are two worth noting: golf and basketball. Both are universally available and can be played by those at almost any skill level and age.

Although it has been said that basketball players are the greatest athletes in the world, anyone can put a hoop in their driveway and shoot the ball. Basketball courts can be found almost anywhere—indoors and outdoors—and anyone who plays can pass or shoot the ball.

Unlike many other sports, golf and basketball can be played alone. With basketball, you do not have to run or pass the ball; you can stand, bounce the ball, and then shoot.

Basketball is accessible to all. Yet while the vast majority of NBA players have dark skin, most of the coaches and team owners do not reflect the players' demographics. Again, this is not a criticism, just a fact based on the statistics of the sport itself.

Those who manage and own the teams are in control, not the players. This is the rule of economics at work.

Golf is a great sport that can be played well into the later years of life, as it is less physically demanding than many other sports. If you have cardiovascular issues or cannot run, you can still participate in golf and be competitive with your peer group. Find a course, and you can play.

On the other hand, can you really?

No! "They" control that too! While golf, like basketball and other sports, is accessible to all and can be played by anyone regardless of their skill level, it is the sacred untouchable that "they" currently, and hope to always, control via courses that are not always accessible because of the price of entry or because they are on private property.

Unlike some other sports, golf is controlled by the rule of economics. If you are a swimmer, you can find a pool, a lake, or even an ocean in which to swim. Convenience and access are factors, but if you can get to a body of water, you can generally swim. If you want to play baseball, basketball, football, soccer, or gymnastics, you must find a place to play. This isn't always easy. You can have the money and desire to play a sport, but it may not be geographically or economically possible.

While many sports and activities are available to all, golf stands unique in that it is not available to all because it is controlled. Most golfers have white skin, notwithstanding geography, as they are controlled by the rule of economics. In many respects, access to golf is controlled by those who make the rules, and to date, 90 percent of professional male golfers have white skin. Yes, there are exceptions, but for the most part, it is a white-dominated sport.

There are other sports examples, and as a society, we accept them not as outliers but as the norm because the sports business is big entertainment. We must not forget who controls the rules of economics and that everyone else is experiencing is the outer limits. Those who make the rules control the game!

11

WHO, THEN, CAN I TRUST?

How many times have you put something away, saying, "I will intentionally place it here, knowing that I will find it?" Then, when you needed the item, you couldn't actually find it? The primary reason is that humans are flawed, imperfect, and living in an imperfect world.

They question of trust is paramount to our individual and corporate success, regardless of what we are trying to achieve. So if we cannot always trust ourselves, or any human being, who can we trust?

Proverbs 3:5 says, "Trust in the LORD with all your heart and lean not on your own understanding."

12

LET GO AND HOLD ON

It is hard to be saved if you are holding on to the very thing holding you back or down. If you are in the water holding on to an anchor, it will be difficult and even impossible for you to be rescued if you are unwilling to let go of the thing you are holding.

In difficult situations, holding on to something like an anchor seems to be best at the time. You need to look for and hold on to an anchor instead of drowning or being lost.

There is a distinction often missed when one is challenged with letting go and being told, "Just hold on!" One must discern if what is being held on to can save or is actually holding you down.

When in the troubled waters of life, indeed you will need something to grab hold of to save yourself and not be lost. Ideas, truths, beliefs, and principles are frontrunners if they have been proven to stand the test of trials over time.

They must also be tested in the context of comfort.

We sometimes do not want to let go, even when we see what has come to rescue or save us, because we want to cling to what is comfortable or familiar. To be saved, we must be willing to let go! We must be willing to let go of what we're holding on to as an anchor.

Comfort and being comfortable are not the issue in and of themselves. The problem is desiring to stay in the context of the familiar.

There are things *known* and things *unknown*. It is the unknown that we often are uncomfortable with, so the thought of moving in the direction of the unknown is discomforting.

The mind may consider the unknown worse than the known. The mind resolves that the known is a familiar friend and the unknown is a foe.

The greatest champion one can have is a voice that says, "Let it go!" Whatever "it" might be, the desire is for you to be truly free.

If "it" is the anchor you are holding on to or the help extended to you that you can't seem to get out of your mind, let go. Let it go so you can be saved, be freed, and truly live.

The unknown you come to know could be your freedom. Moreover, if letting go does not result in your freedom, you are at least freed from the old and released into something new. The unknown then becomes the known we prefer. It's the familiar. Even if we find ourselves saying, "I hate this," we tend to discard what we hate only when it appears something better is being offered.

Letting go of the unknown is much easier than letting go of the known. However, often there is much more than meets the eye in the unknown, and it is discovered only when you let go of the known.

Being set free in this manner plays out largely when compassion comes calling and we help others.

The unknown we most often are resistant to is the act of giving. Letting things go actually frees and even saves the giver. The giver is freed from being possessive and saved from the destiny of those who care only about themselves and the temporal.

✶ ✶ ✶ ✶ ✶

Consider the following. This person wanted to be saved, but when faced with the requirement to let go, that fear of the unknown kept him bound in his life of familiarity and comfort.

A rich man once asked, "What must I do to be saved?" Jesus' first response was that he must keep the commandments given. The rich person said, "I have done all of these things," but Jesus said, "You still lack one thing. Sell everything you have and give to the poor." (See Luke 18:18–30 for the entire account.)

What did Jesus say? "Sell everything you have, give to the poor, and you will have treasure in heaven. Then come, follow Me."

You may think, "Hold on, did I hear you correctly? Am I to sell everything I have and give to the poor, and then I will have treasures in heaven?"

Does Jesus really expect or require us to sell everything we have, give to the poor, and follow Him? The answer is yes. Nevertheless, hold on. Notice something important—the subtle difference is two words: *you have.*

Consider exactly what was said—the known: "Sell everything you have and give to the poor." Now consider the unknown, what you *heard*, or *how you interpreted* what you heard: "Sell everything and give it to the poor." Selling everything *you have* is much different from selling everything.

If you realize that everything *you have* has been given to you and is not yours, then *you* genuinely have nothing to sell—the known. Consider the unknown that could have set the man free: Sell everything you profess to own and give it to the poor. Manage what has been given to you according to God's standards.

Letting go of everything you have and holding on to what God has given you to manage is the greatest freedom a person can experience in life.

This is powerful, as it defines what we should be doing and what we must rid ourselves of that is unproductive or harmful. Anything that we are unwilling to let go of, believing it is ours, is most often weighing us down and serving as an anchor.

The wonderful thing we can know from this account is the unknown. In letting go of the known familiar, we have a promise regarding the unknown that we can hold on to regardless of circumstances. Such promises regarding the unknown cancel the risks we believe we face in embracing the unfamiliar.

Depart from the familiar known into the unknown to save you from yourself. It is a worthwhile, fulfilling, life-changing experience on earth, with the promise of something even greater waiting after your last breath.

——————— 13 ———————

SAVE ME FROM ME

W E KNOW WHEN something is *wrong*, or at least we know when something is not *right*. As we view the world through the lens of sensibility and consider each person and his or her diverse background, there remains much that virtually everyone dislikes (if it were possible for everyone to agree). Often our actions result in unintended consequences, and we say one must live with those consequences one way or another.

We pronounce that we are evolving and those who are ignorant shall be left behind. Those who proclaim our society is evolving do so based on two premises:

1. We must always be learning and accepting of new things.

2. If there is a reality, it is relative to evolution or the evolved.

Because of these premises, humans do not want to face reality or be told of their condition, even with the solution or cure at hand. It was said some time ago and holds true today, "They will be ever learning but never coming into the knowledge of the *truth*; otherwise, they would turn, and I would heal them."[1] At this point, we may need to be rescued from ourselves.

——————— 14 ———————

CHILDREN, HOW LITTLE THEY KNOW

C HILDREN, WHAT DO they know? Put several babies in a room together, and the most profound thing you will see is that without any outside influence, in short order, each one will grab what they want.

They will even fight for what they want. "I want it; it's mine; give it to me," they would say if they could talk, but this is expressed in their actions. Innocent as they are, babies do what babies do. They innately care primarily about themselves

Follow that same group of babies, who are driven primarily by their self-interest, and as they grow, they recognize that the world is larger than they are. Put that group back in the same room as young children. While their first instinct is to look out for themselves, a phenomenon unfolds. When they see one of their peers in need, they share from what they have. If that peer is struggling, they offer a helping hand with no regard to skin color or physical differences. *Children, how little they know!*

Over time, the children in the room find themselves simply being children, caring less about selfish needs and more about being together. They think, "All is good; therefore, I will share what I have." *Children, how little they know!*

If we keep looking, we see an amazing thing: One child would sip on a bottle of soda or a cup of juice, then stop and offer it to the person next to them. The other child would take it, sip a little, and then share it with another, and so on. Remember, they are only children. They do so only to share or have what the other has, nothing more. *Children, how little they know!*

We find these children sharing among themselves. Though some need a little nudging, none has worries about drinking from the same bottle or picking up germs. *Children, how little they know!*

They are happy, not just in themselves but in sharing, mostly giving no care to sharing, even if one child took from another. Remember, they are children, and though they may cry, they usually get over it quickly! It is rare to see a child *give* something to another child and then cry. *Children, how little they know!*

The natural behaviors we call human nature continue until they are influenced by human deficiencies and disregard for the Creator. Children, protective of themselves but willing to share, usually share until stopped by some outside influence. In our fallen humanness, instead of propagating or facilitating this innocence, we pollute it with our defects and insert that defective mindset into the innocent.

Seeds of hate and dislike of anything different are planted into the innocent. Unfortunately for the children, who were created to propagate truth reflecting their Creator, they have now been altered. The course has been interrupted and distorted by corrupted, damaged characters, who manipulate others with misguided, guided precision. The seeds planted are then mutated into the children, replicating the unnatural outside influences imposed upon them: hatred, dislike, and notice of differences. This is done so easily because they are children. *Children, how little they know!*

With little choice or desire in the matter, the innocent have been infected and affected to the point that what was once naturally experienced among them—sharing, caring, and empathy—is now a thing of the past. How can this happen? *Children, how little they know.*

The children did not make the choice. The innocent, uninformed, uninfluenced choice the children made was first to be selfish. They innately realized that selfishness and lack of empathy for someone in need is not life-sustaining, natural, or a basic instinct

Children, how little they know until they are taught, or as some might say, until they learn. How little damage can a child do until they are influenced? *Children, how little they know!*

The children made distinctions only when they were infected by outside, compromising influences. Children, what do they know? They know to love and share and that they cannot exist independently. They know as children that they can hurt no more or less than the next child because all of them are similar but different. They are unaffected, innocent children until they have been infected by the affected defective!

Children, what do they know? If only they knew and had the power to stay away from the infected and defective, or to free themselves from those who seek to make them in their own defective, infected image. *But children, how little they know!*

Children, what do they know? The children, indeed, know much. Sadly, though, because they are children, we don't seek to learn what they can teach us.

Children, what do they know? They know and can teach us that they have no problem being around people who are different, and we should learn to do the same.

Children, what do they know? They know a child may dislike or reject a drink or a particular food because of personal taste, but rarely has a child or toddler rejected another child. They innocently trust those who "look like them," meaning other children who come in all shapes, sizes, and colors.

Children, what do they know? Do they know what to reject? How can they know? *Children, how little they know!*

Children, how little they know the little they know. There is much we can learn from how little they know!

— 15 —

NAKED AND AFRAID

UNLESS WE ARE forced to coexist, why do we tend to feel comfortable and only want to be with people who look like us or whom we can identify with?

We often relax our defenses with those who look like us and have raised walls when we are with those who are different. This seems to be truer with a particular group of people; specifically, it is more typical for the affluent to fit this category. Having, achieving, and enjoying are possible when those who can identify with one another are together. It is in the totality of that environment that the affluent are most comfortable.

Profoundly, what is in pursuit of being comfortable—always shadowing and following—is being uncomfortable. Having subtlety seems to bring a sense of discomfort rather than comfort. The *haves* would say, "I thought that by having stuff, I would be completely comfortable. Why am I so uneasy, always looking over my shoulders and watching where I park? My guard is more up than it is down!

"I notice that one of the main things that make me uncomfortable is being around those I cannot identify with because we don't look alike. I don't look like them, and they don't look like me. Because we don't look like each other, I don't want to be around them.

"Not liking others is making me uncomfortable. How can this be? I'm living a life of great comfort! With all I have, all I know, and all I can do, what on earth could possibly make me uncomfortable, uneasy, or afraid?"

What makes us afraid? We are only at ease when we return to those with whom we are familiar, *those with whom we identify!*

When you are naked, you will be afraid!

A Rich Man's Story: The Life of Comfort and Fear

I'm on my way home after a long day of work. Being on a plane for several hours is a bummer, even if you are in first class. I would have been on the company's private jet if not for recent budget cuts. No TSA, metal detectors, kids, or crowds, and a car waiting when I step off the jet stairs is always my preference.

I'm thankful for what I have, but traveling is still exhausting. Fortunately, I have hired a private car to get me home because I'm too tired to drive. Now, I only have to sit back patiently while the driver navigates the traffic. Perhaps to ease my nerves from a long day, I will have a cocktail; the driver should have noted my preferences when I booked the car.

As we wind through the busy streets, I look at the places of commerce and the neighborhoods that I'm thankful I didn't have to grow up in. Then we pass by the area where I did spend my childhood, and I'm grateful that I can say I *used to* live there.

The quietness of the car, the great music, and the glass of wine calm me from a long, stressful week. As we pass each block, I cannot help but notice the masses crossing in opposing directions, some pressed in groups but all seemingly going somewhere and nowhere at the same time. "At least they look busy," I think.

At some stop lights amid the heavy traffic, a few people look to see who is inside my shining black limo with tinted windows. I can see them looking, but thankfully they cannot see me. Although insulated, I find it somewhat unnerving that people try to invade my privacy.

Never ungrateful, I am thankful I am not in the crowds and am anxious to get home to my sanctuary of peace and the familiar. I hope and pray there will be few red lights. I find myself especially asking God that nothing will go wrong with the car, as the last two limo trips were a disaster—no AC in one, and a ride so rough in the other, I was sure we were riding on a flat tire. Both limos got me home safely, but I was worried.

Thirty minutes go by, and the scenery begins to change, indicating we are getting closer to my home, my refuge, and my family. Few people are outside these days. Lush, green trees; beautiful flowers; and lakes replace sidewalks and trash on the streets, and yet few people are outside.

After traveling from the airport through the city, seeing the familiar gate to my neighborhood gives me a sense of relief. I unlock the car door once we pass the security guard in anticipation of a quick exit. I finally begin to let my guard down. I think I can sense my heart rate and blood pressure going down.

When I arrive home, I have to disarm the alarm system. Once inside, I arm it again, turning on the security system to see and hear the outside. Now that I am at home, I am no longer afraid.

I never thought to question why I would turn off my alarm system, enter my home, and turn it back on while living in a gated community.

An Interview With Afraid

Interviewer: "Why are you afraid? You're in the comfort of your own home, in your world, which is filled with fewer worries than most. And yet..."

Afraid: "Well, maybe I'm not afraid. Maybe I realize that I've worked hard and earned a certain lifestyle. I deserve to be away from a world that, frankly, is not living. I have mine, and if I can only enjoy it in my world, then so be it! I have the money. There are others like me, though few in number, whom I can spend time with! I can't risk being around people who hate me because of what I have or try to take it from me. They have not earned it and, in my mind, don't deserve it. I will not take the risk of being around such people."

Unstated Confession—I Am Afraid

Why do you feel afraid? Because you are naked and exposed.

This exposure is not intended to embarrass but to reveal that you need covering so you will no longer be afraid.

Your possessions, power, and position cannot cover your exposure; they only amplify the fact that the product of your own hands cannot adequately cover you.

You are afraid because you are naked.

———— 16 ————

IMAGE IS EVERYTHING

THE MOST EFFECTIVE way to keep a person bound is to constantly remind them of their past offenses and sins. Who is the master at this? The accuser of the brothers!

In 2021, and in previous decades, we continually talked about and did the same things. In doing so, we reminded ourselves of the same old same old. It's old, not new. Perhaps it's not insanity, as some people truly *do not* want things to change.

There appears to be competing truths: "If you forget the past, you are prone to repeat it." Elsewhere it is said, "Forget the past and strain toward what is ahead." Both are true; however, they must be interpreted with a desire to understand their application.

The first example implies that we do not forget past transgressions and what provoked them. Therefore, do not make the same mess by repeating the action. The second says to stop bringing up the past except if there's a direct, positive connection to what is ahead. There must be a good, profitable, productive reason for bringing up the past. Negative past events serve only as reminders of who and where we once were, with an eye toward forgetting. We know there is a problem when we are continually reminded of negative past actions committed by society; it means past mistakes have not gone away. We continue to bring them up!

The answer is to eliminate, not repeat. To talk about the new is to talk about the solution.

We rarely talk about the new, the perfect picture, and the process to get to the best. Where is that image, given that we now know that image is everything?

Television promotes images that divide. Most conversations remind us of past and current divisions without portraying the image of unity.

Blended families are not the answer, as differences are to be celebrated, *not* blended so they disappear.

The villain in the movie *The Incredibles* has a great line: "When everyone's super, no one will be."[1] If we make everyone the same, blending away our differences, the differences can no longer be super.

Each person or group is super on his or her own and should be celebrated. It will be difficult and perhaps even impossible to celebrate if everything is the same.

Blending families and cultures can be a part of the whole but should not be the whole. If everything is blended, nothing is unique or different and worth celebrating.

Many have heard of the tower of Babel. It led to the creation of differences and separation.

It is comical to see people thinking they can right wrongs that have brought division and create a perfect world by accepting everything. Through this acceptance, they imagine differences can be blended so there are none.

There is no need for a new world, touted to be progressive in the name of diversity, inclusion, belonging, and acceptance. The human race has always been made of people with unique differences. It is these differences that make the human race human.

The vast differences portrayed in humans fail miserably at accurately reflecting the image of God, even though we are made in His image. This should be to no one's surprise since God is infinite. Image is everything!

--- **17** ---

WHAT WE'VE GOT HERE ...

ONE OF THE most memorable lines in the 1967 film *Cool Hand Luke* is a truth everyone should note: "What we've got here is failure to communicate!"[1]

In the world of technology, many units must communicate with one another for the system to work correctly. The same occurs in relationships. When we fail or cease to communicate, things will be out of sync, and the system will not work as designed.

———————— 18 ————————

WE NEED MI, NOT AI

W^E NEED *MIRRORED* Intelligence, not artificial intelligence. Our silent but overtly sought desire to be like God has spiraled out of control and unleashed incalculable harm, an unintended consequence.

Authentic intelligence is simply a mirror of true intelligence. Progress would not attempt to supplant truth by bending the rules or trying to redefine that which is not truly intelligent.

In the year 2020, COVID-19 proved to the world that visiting people remotely is no substitute for human touch. An authentic connection cannot be sustained through artificial means, no matter how intelligent the tools.

AI continues to prove itself artificial, and it can hardly be considered intelligent. New terms are being introduced into society. These words and ideologies are rightfully called artificial, but they lack intelligence. It would be more appropriate for AI to be called artificially sought intelligence, or hoped-for or believed-to-be intelligence. AI is exactly what its name proclaims: *artificial* intelligence.

The popular acronyms in our society are equally artificial. They steal from or seek to redefine the original, resulting in terms such as trans, same-sex, and nonbinary. The artificial has no limits and continues to expand, producing a steady stream of new identities.

Original intelligence cannot be replicated, reproduced, or copied. If we want to make progress, intelligence cannot originate with us. We are flawed, and intelligence based on the flawed cannot reach beyond the flawed.

There is intelligence that is proven and has stood the test of time. It continues to present itself as real and not artificial, and when accessed, it can advance and even exceed man's ambition. We must *mirror* it. We must look deeply into what has been proven true and stay disciplined to its rules. Only then can we enjoy a life beyond our imaginations—one that is not artificial but real.

What the world needs is mirrored intelligence, an intelligence that is not artificial and does not require interpretation. Consider the impact of mirroring true intelligence: When you see your brother or sister in need, if you have this world's possessions, you have compassion on them and help them.

Ancient wisdom would say if you don't love those whom you do see, how can you say you love God, whom you don't see? If all of us who have something would do our part for those we see, wars, hunger, conflict, and lack would not be able to sprout.

The problem is that a majority of people don't see it that way! Instead of mirroring true intelligence, they want to address the issues of this world artificially through their own interpretation of intelligence.

AI is presented as a pinnacle of human achievement, with an eye toward achieving heights and benefits one could only dream of. Spanning the endless reaches of our universe, AI would bring the unthinkable and unattainable into reality, though artificially. After all, who would want the real thing in a world bent on suppressing the truth!

Is it possible for the created to surpass the creator? Is it possible for the imperfect to create perfection?

Genetically modified organisms and the artificial enhancements that are supposed to benefit us have, in fact, proven almost without exception to do the opposite. And the original is almost always preferred over the altered.

The original cannot be perfected, as it is already perfect. Any so-called improvements only take away. In these cases, more is less. The more we call ourselves progressive or advancing by altering the original, the less we progress or advance. We need not evolve except to evolve from believing the false to embracing the truth.

EXAMINATION

What We See Is Not Always the Truth

WE FREQUENTLY MAKE decisions based on what we believe to be true, only to find out later that we were completely mistaken. That's because what we see is not always the truth.

The comic book character Superman had X-ray vision, which allowed him to see beyond the surface to what was inside. Unfortunately, we don't possess that superpower and are forced to make judgments and life decisions based on what we can see, experience, or glean from outside sources.

In this section, we will examine what it means to look beyond the surface of important issues to unearth the truth.

—— **19** ——

THE QUEST FOR PEACE: PEACE OF MIND

THE FOLLOWING ENTRY reflects comments collected over time from various people in different occupations. Although the word *peace* is rarely used explicitly, it is always the intended goal.

It is necessary to define certain terms in advance so there is an understanding of how those terms are applied. It is not necessary to agree with the definitions, positions, or conclusions presented, but the definitions provide a base of knowledge.

- *Haves*—those who have power, possessions, and platforms

- *Have-nots*—those who have little say, few possessions, and no power, not even the perceived power from voting; they are pawns on the chessboard of our society

- Peace—the absence of conflict, uneasiness, trouble, volatility, turbulence, disagreement, or dislike

*** * * * ***

Peace is what everyone desires and seeks. "Better a crumb with peace than a fattened calf with strife," according to ancient wisdom.[1]

It has been said that everyone wants one thing: peace of mind. If people were given just one choice, most would say, "More than anything, let me be at peace."

It could be said that with the absence of war around us or struggle within us, there would be peace.

An interesting and mysterious statement is found in an ancient proverb: "A poor man hears no threats."[2] One interpretation is that when a person has little to nothing that can be taken, they have nothing to lose and don't feel the threat of harm.

POOR

When they're not living in fear of loss, people find themselves at peace by not having to protect, defend, or fight to keep anything, at least not from a surface view. It can be said that the poor don't own anything. As troubled as they may be, the poor have less to worry over than those who have. In this way, the poor are closer to peace than those who have. The poor—the *have-nots*—seek foremost to be satisfied by having their needs met. The *haves* can rarely be satisfied. As much as they have, they seem to never be at peace.

The *haves* seek peace, as do the *have-nots*. The *haves* possess some things that present themselves as giving or paving the way to peace. But they are deceived. The *have-nots* have little to nothing and resolve that by getting something—even just one thing, such as much-needed food or drink—they will gain some sense of peace. The *haves* also believe that they want only their needs met. However, they claim to need many things to have peace and happiness.

If they attain what they seek, both groups say, "I have what I need, and therefore, not being in need, I am at peace!" For most, peace is the absence of conflict or lack of that which is contrary, disliked, or unwanted.

PAIN

We often seek what we want instead of what we need, so our lack of peace results from not getting what we want rather than not getting what we need. For the poor, lacking necessities is the root of their pain. Conversely, the wealthy experience pain from not attaining more of what they want. It is important to understand that people are not poor simply because they are not financially rich but because their needs are unmet. One group feels pain because their needs are not met while the other feels pain because their wants are not satisfied.

People often believe that material things will give them a worry-free life. They think, "If only I had this or that, I would be better off and not under stress. I would be at peace." This often happens when someone does not have what is needed and others do. One group might say, "You have a house; I don't. You have a car; I don't." Someone who has their needs met but not their wants might say, "You have a bigger house; mine is too small. You have a newer car; mine is outdated." For true peace to occur, a distinction must be made between needs and wants. Surprisingly, the poor are often better than the rich at distinguishing between needs and wants, because they are faced with needs daily.

PLAUSIBLE

The wise, through their experience, say less is more. They know that for many of us, it is better to have less rather than more to manage. Having things takes energy and involves work, and it can become stressful to maintain what we have attained; therefore, having material possessions can ultimately rob one of peace. This reasoning suggests that not having material things creates a better opportunity for someone to be at peace.

Suggesting that it is better to have little or nothing proposes that a person will be at peace because they possess little to nothing and therefore have nothing to worry about. However, it is unreasonable to think someone should be at peace just because they lack what they need.

PLURAL

Is it possible to be needy and at peace at the same time? Perhaps the first step in attaining a sense of peace is to realize that peace is not found solely in having things.

When someone has material possessions or information that could benefit others, an expectation is placed upon them. Those with possessions, power, and platforms must try to address others' needs. When practiced, this is the pathway to peace for both those who have and those in need. Failed efforts are better than no effort.

20

THE QUEST FOR PEACE: THE PIECE IGNORED

UNREST AND UNEASINESS are the products of conflict resulting from a significant piece missing in our society.

PRESSURE

Most people want and seek peace. The conflict around us reflects what is happening inside us, and what is happening inside fuels the outside. Conflict is the disrupter of peace. One person can be at peace, but if another is not, there will be conflict and, therefore, no peace.

Being conflicted often results from not realizing or accepting the responsibilities of having or not having something. It has been said that ignorance is no excuse, and that is certainly true in this case.

PATTERN

Ignorance is likely not the issue, as most people can perceive when something is wrong. A person can ignore a thing because he or she is insulated. "I'm at peace having; you are not at peace in not having. But I ignore the fact that society generally is not at peace! But I am at peace, or I have a sense of being at peace. Life around me lacks peace, but my world has a slice of peace in it, and if I do not experience the bad piece of life, I am at peace."

In the theater of life, neither ignoring a matter nor inexperience makes it go away. Instead, it magnifies it as they both take on the spotlight. The existence of those at peace amid society's chaos is the missing piece that explains why there is uneasiness and unrest.

The missing piece involves two scenarios: peace as a result of being insulated from conflict, or no peace as a result of being isolated in conflict. The missed piece is that the insulated and the isolated want the same things as others, but they are being kept from it.

PERHAPS

We can debate the idea that both the *haves* and *have-nots* are looking for the same thing. Perhaps to quiet the matter, it can be said that we are the same but different. We are not all capable of doing the same things, as no two people are exactly alike, but we all are capable of something. Thus, each of us is different. What unifies mankind is that we all seek something, and the desire and pursuit of those things make us all the same. Not attaining is the source of conflict, the disrupter of peace.

POTENTIAL

The missed piece ignored by some and experienced by others is that both the *haves* and *have-nots* can achieve and attain peace if they go about it the right way. The challenge, however, is often related to things such as possessions, information, power, and access—or the lack thereof—which can determine the outcome.

The saying "with much power comes much responsibility" has merit, as does an older saying, "Of the one who has much, much is expected, required, demanded."[1]

Is it reasonable to accept that having something (regardless of how it was attained—whether imputed, given, worked for, or stolen) resolves the conflict that those who don't have face daily? Having should satisfy the downside of not having, which is often the lack of peace, but that is not always the case. Sometimes just the opposite is true.

PROBABLE

The responsibilities that are foundational to peace are a powerful force and deserve our attention.

Consider that if you have a thing that is not wanted, you can get rid of it and in doing so, potentially fulfill your obligation or reason for being given abundance. For some, it was given because they are givers. However, there never seem to be enough willing givers to address the multitude of unmet needs of those who don't have enough.

The majority of people seem to base peace in their personal world on what they can or cannot attain, and yet even when they have their piece of that pie, they often find no peace in it at all.

———————— 21 ————————

THE QUEST FOR PEACE: PICTURE NOT PERFECT PERFECTED

MANY OF THE *haves* just happen to be our lawmakers and attorneys. This is an interesting reality, since they directly create, confirm, and help enforce the rules by which both *haves* and *have-nots* are bound to obey.

PRESENTATION

The *haves*, who are the minority, make laws for the majority and live in communities that look very different from the communities of those for whom they make rules.

The workplace is similar though there are differences. The *haves* and *have-nots* may work for the same company, but the working conditions and regulations differ for each group. These facts, among others, are presented to the masses as the way of life. These incongruities are the never-to-be-defeated enemies of peace.

PROCLAMATION

The *haves* live in exclusive communities, dine at choice spots, travel on private jets, drive luxury cars, run businesses, have yachts and other motorized toys, and often own multiple residences. "We have earned it," most would say. "Through hard work, we have earned the right to enjoy this lifestyle!"

PRODIGIOUS

Most of the *haves* look at their net worth or personal balance sheets and see that, as a proverb encourages, they have amassed enough wealth for their children's children.[1] Retirement is not a worry, as their retirement funds, pension plans, stocks, properties, and other investments derived from excelling in business are prodigious.

PERPLEXING

What happens when someone is prodigious? They have enough for their children's children but not enough to help anyone else's children.

PICTURE

The *haves* are a diverse group. They enjoy power, access, authority, and various levels of wealth. Some *haves* may not boast great material wealth but still wield power. The *haves* are found in government, nonprofit associations, and even faith-based organizations, though to a lesser degree. The overwhelming majority of the *haves* are in business and government.

The *haves* can boast of having money in the bank, and their most significant worry is maintaining good financial and physical health to enjoy the fruits of having.

PUZZLING

Of course, the *haves* are not worry-free. There is a missing piece in their peace. They would say that protecting, preserving, and growing wealth is more of a burden than most realize. The *haves* are not immune to end-of-life realities and the need to ensure that what has been amassed is protected, to ensure that what they've started continues and does not fall into the wrong hands. The *have-nots* often cannot identify with this piece of the puzzle.

The burden of the *haves* is more than what meets the eye, for an extravagant lifestyle brings more to manage. Someone is always after their money, seeking gifts and donations to various causes. These requests often are unreasonable and disrupt the *haves'* peace.

The question that comes with having is, "How can I responsibly meet my own needs, then my family's, then others' without losing sight of the primary goal?"

"Yes," some would say "having is truly a burden, but isn't the alternative a burden too? Better to have than not to have! Who would argue that one is better off being disturbed by having than not being disturbed but also not having?" It's a puzzling situation either way.

POSSIBLE

Is it possible that there is little peace in having and no real peace without having? It is a difficult choice to have peace that carries the burden of having things, or to have peace that brings the burden of being in need. It can be a dilemma if you are sincerely seeking real peace.

PREPOSTEROUS

The *haves* carry many burdens. A major burden is to manage the who's who, the decision-makers, lawmakers, and policy-shapers who can help protect what the *haves* have amassed and ensure their families' futures. The *haves* must manage those who make laws that affect the *have-nots* much more than the *haves*, and they realize how much responsibility and power they have been given.

PASSING PEACE

Peace can be passed on or forfeited. The only time it seems the *haves* would miss an opportunity to pass it on is when they fail to take ownership of the opportunity.

A significant difference between the *haves* and the *have-nots* is access. The *haves* are fortunate to hold the benefit of access. They help the powerbrokers, and the powerbrokers help the *haves*. In this way, they feed each other. The *have-nots* are the recipients of what the powerbrokers impose on them. They work, trying to survive, and sometimes are barely able to help themselves, much less one another.

PONTIFICATING

Who would argue that being a *have* is not necessarily a dream come true, no matter where you are on the globe? Isn't having a thing to enjoy, far better than suffering and going without?

INSIDE THE BUBBLE

Only when the *haves* go home to their gated communities can they let down their guard a little and enjoy the fruits of their labor. They view what they have earned with a sense of thanksgiving and pride. But they also have an uneasiness or fear of the woes affecting those outside their affluent bubble. This bubble might burst one day, or the gates may not hold. "We have our battles to survive, and we cannot engage in yours and ours at the same time," say the *haves*.

The *haves* would never stoop so low as to steal a car or jewels from their neighbors' homes. In fact, the *haves* look out for one another, especially when it comes to enjoying the fruits of their labor and the privilege that comes with it. The *haves* do not consider having as a responsibility but a privilege.

The *haves* may say of themselves: "It is unthinkable—even preposterous—to suggest that a have would ever cheat, break laws, bend the rules, put others down, or squeeze all the juice out of the orange just because there is something left to squeeze out. No, the *haves* would never engage in insider trading, preferential treatment, or the strategic hiring or promotion of certain people. Why on earth would a have even consider such things when they have already attained so much?"

They might say:

> Such acts could be defined as anarchy, but a *have* would never engage in that kind of behavior! Such acts demonstrate a lack of control. People who behave in such a manner are not worthy of having things or leading others.
>
> A *have* would never be connected to or in support of rioting. It seems impossible for the *haves* to identify with minorities. But the one minority group they identify with is their own group—the *haves*. There are significantly more *haves*-nots than *haves*.
>
> A *have* has never and would never take another *have* to court in protest of a violation. A *have* would never sell off assets or transfer holdings to another company if that meant knowingly tearing down what they built or hope to attain.

The *haves* are not only above reproach but also above the actions of the *have-nots*. It is the *have-nots* who are predisposed to acting in a manner the *haves* could not and would not condescend to engage in.

We, the *haves*, do not work in city streets and among those we feel we are better than others. We, the *haves*, are not urban; we are not suburban. We are only urban when the *have-nots* are absent from urban areas. We are only suburban when the *have-nots* are absent from the suburban areas. If they occupy both spaces, we create our own space. Each group should have its own space. We respect them, and they respect us.

We, the *haves*, create prestigious spaces with names such as the Hamptons, Beverly Hills, and Martha's Vineyard. The beachfront properties, high-rises, private islands, and exclusive communities; Rodeo Drive; Magnificent Mile; Millionaires' Row—these are our safe havens.

We see that the word *haven* is made up of the word *have*. I have things that provide my safe haven. These havens are purchased by the *haves* as places of refuge and rest so we can be at peace.

We, the *haves*, were made for this. We have earned it. We deserve it; the *have-nots* do not. We, the *haves*, are not like the *have-nots*. We don't do what they do; we don't act the way they act; we don't aspire to what they aspire. We are different. It is not skin color, culture, tongue, or birth (aside from those born into royalty) that brings the separation. Our distinction is based upon what one has or doesn't have.

PERFECT

Is there a distinction between the *haves* and *have-nots*? Yes! Yet while very different, they are also similar in many ways.

It is easy and convenient to cover up what both have in common. It takes great effort to convince the *have-nots* that they are more like the *haves* than different. Both groups seek peace and believe the wide road to finding peace is in "having."

For the *haves*, though, there is a distinct difference. The *haves* believe that having makes them innately different from the *have-nots*. "Because we are the *haves*, we are better than the *have-nots*," they might think or even say out loud.

The difference, however, is that some people have an abundance, but most do not. Just because you have does not mean you are better than those who do not have abundance.

"We will not be likened to them," the *haves* say. "We are most certainly different from those *have-nots*, who are less-than based upon how little they have."

Plausible

"We are better than that!" say the *haves* as they peer into the lives of the *have-nots*. "We teach our children better, don't we? We fund think tanks, projects, and universities to better mankind. We send employees and even family members to underserved places. We direct our business to communities and nations that need development (and they just so happen to charge less to produce goods, are free from regulations, and are willing to do almost anything for little to no pay).

"We send jobs to those who have been denied the opportunity. We expect the *have-nots* to accept our goodwill humbly and gratefully. We, the *haves*, are role models, the best citizens on earth. We do what serves us best to keep our peace and be at peace!"

The *haves* don't say this outright, but their actions loudly say: "We do what we do. It is who we are, and it is why we have." It is clear that the *haves* believe they are more deserving of good things than the *have-nots* are.

It is inconceivable—impossible—as it would be crossing the line to suggest or even think that a *have* could stoop to the level of a *have-not* and hurt those around them. Not all *haves* look to harm the *have-nots*; some harm is inadvertent. Are the *have-nots* impacted because of the *haves'* ignorance, or is it arrogance?

Panic

It is not enough for the *have-nots* to suffer solely because they do not have. They also must fight the *haves*, the obstacles in power preventing them from obtaining.

The *haves* would proclaim they are engaged in dual fights. This is not outright, but they fight to stay away from the *have-nots*, and they fight to have and maintain their position of power.

"We fight corporately in our boardrooms to advance and defend our financial objectives," they would say. "And socially, we must defend ourselves from the *have-nots*, who serve us concerning those same objectives. We, the *haves*, will never find ourselves in the alleys, the streets, the underground, the slums, the gutter, or the overpopulated, underserved cities that plague society."

The *haves* often feel above reproach and worthy of being followed. "We, the *haves*, never work in dark alleys, backrooms, basements, underground tunnels, or any place that even remotely looks like a hiding place. We, the *haves*, do our work in our executive offices, courtrooms, and boardrooms, and at meetings with policy- and decision-makers. We take pride in the places where we do our most excellent work in shaping society, unlike the *have-nots*, who hide.

"We, the *haves*, would not do anything in the dark so it's hidden. We are so proficient in what we do that we can do it in broad daylight. And being among peers, we get a pass, a nod, and forgiveness, since the *haves* are brothers. Thus, we do not need to hide! Our actions are not characterized as crimes (though they often are) because we will get what we want and protect what is ours by any means necessary." This is understood, accepted, and defended by the *haves*.

Pain

More damage has likely been done in society by the *haves* committing white-collar crimes and through their narcissistic mismanagement of resources than through the collective failed attempts of the *have-nots*. It may not sound plausible to a *have*, who would immediately try to defend their group, but even they know it's likely more true than not.

PRINCIPLE

As a result of not having, the *have-nots* contribute to the lack of peace in our society by trying, by any means necessary, to cease being a *have-not*. Here is a question to consider, "If you don't trade goods, you will trade in conflict?"

PERFECT

While the *haves*, and to a lesser degree the *have-nots*, have contributed to the lack of peace in society by their actions, the *haves* bear a greater responsibility to heal societal ills and advance the cause of both groups. It is the duty and reasonable mission of the *haves* to work tirelessly toward seeing that the *have-nots* become *haves* as well, because by doing so, the new *haves* would be making positive contributions as well. There would be much more peace and security in all our lives.

It stands to reason that because the *haves* enjoy privileges that *have-nots* do not, they have a larger degree of responsibility to help improve the lives of the whole. Having privileges and resources out of the reach of others brings with it the requirements and expectations that peacemaking demands.

Not taking this responsibility seriously, or taking no action at all, simply leads to no peace at all, and everyone suffers as a result.

—————————— 22 ——————————

WHO IS MY NEIGHBOR?

Neighbor: a person who lives near another; a person or thing near another; one's fellow human being.

I F WE CALL someone a neighbor, the term suggests we have a connection to those we encounter where we live. Further, the term implies we are more than simply aware of someone's existence. The saying "I am my brother's keeper" means we care about and serve those we are privileged to dwell among, with a greater emphasis on those in need. They are our neighbors.

However, we often decide who we want to be our neighbors and who makes up our neighborhood. We may look around and say, "Never! I will never land in that neighborhood where 'they' are."

Where are they? They live in the neighborhood I call "Neighbor-Neverland"! It is a land that defines the relational and defies the physical.

Exploring the Neighborhood of *Neighbor-Neverland*

This is the talk about *Neighbor-Neverland*.

> I don't have neighbors—I have people around me whom I either accept or deem unacceptable. They are not neighbors, as I don't need or desire neighbors. Those whom I accept I will embrace and engage. Those who are not acceptable, I will not embrace or engage. Who I accept and who I reject determines who I consider my neighbor. I recognize that being a neighbor carries responsibility. Therefore, I choose who gets to be my neighbor and do so with careful discrimination.

Life in Neighbor-Neverland—Who Is My Neighbor?

A dark-skinned person opened a retail store in an affluent area to serve his neighbors, who lived close or far. Whoever would visit, he would embrace. His reason for going into business was to meet needs and make a profit.

He knew the primary customer base was not dark-skinned but people whose skin color was much lighter than his own. The differences in skin color and economic status mattered little to this business owner, as his focus was meeting their needs and treating all with the highest level of care. His vision was to bring the best products and services to his customers; after all, the business was in their community, and they were his neighbors.

The dark-skinned business owner opened the doors with joy and optimism, anticipating he would serve all who came. He was glad to serve those in the community, as they were his neighbors.

The business opened without fanfare, and people came as he had hoped, buying goods and experiencing what patrons described as exceptional service. The owner was elated, taking pride in the positive word on the street about his business, as he had invested much time and money in its launch. While proud that he opened the store and thankful for the response, he never told anyone he was the owner.

Although the store owner never publicized his identity, the customers discovered who owned the store. When those whom the store owner considered his neighbors found the store was owned by a dark-skinned person, sales mysteriously dropped. The word on the street changed from "exceptional" to "there are other options."

Many who became aware of the owner did not return and shared the news of the owner's skin color. Over time, sales dried up. Facing bankruptcy, the owner and his wife began arguing over money. They knew they were facing closure, and a discussion of divorce arose. The once-proud store owners were now humiliated. Being proud, they continued to fight. However, after a while, with little good news and virtually no sales, the owners saw the writing on the wall and knew they needed to close the doors.

The employees contributed to the decision to close the store. Once some of the staff knew who owned the store, their work habits and attitudes changed. They required more management because they worked less and complained more. Later it was discovered that some employees were online looking for other employment while on the job. This discovery was the final nail in the coffin.

One may think this is just a story, a work of fiction. This type of thing could not possibly happen. But could it?

Some may think, "Never has a dark-skinned person walked into a bank and a white-skinned person denied them a loan, charged them a higher interest rate, or required them to jump through more hoops than usual. Never has a dark-skinned person, after being pre-qualified, been denied what was offered to those with a different skin color or social status, even if they were next-door neighbors.

"Never has a dark-skinned person, or someone without the socially acceptable skin color, been detained for no reason but simply because.

Never has a dark-skinned person been treated differently because of what they do *not* look like."

It's easy to think this. After all, this is Neighbor-Neverland.

However, by traveling and exploring the neighborhood of Neighbor-Neverland, we realize these things take place.

This is where it must be asked, "In Neighbor-Neverland, who is my neighbor?"

In Neighbor-Neverland, if you don't look, act, and believe like the people around you, even though you live next to them, work side by side, or even serve in the same military fighting a common enemy, you are not their neighbor! This is, after all, Neighbor-Neverland.

In some cases, it seems as if it's not about the money, even though it always is about the money. In Neighbor-Neverland, money is spent only with those with whom one wants to spend their money. One may have thought money is money. However, in Neighbor-Neverland, it is said, "We will buy from you when, how, and only as we decree."

The entrepreneurs who closed the business considered that their skin color might have been a factor in the hardship of the business. What they did not realize is that a dark-skinned person attempting something (starting a business, etc.) in a neighborhood made up mostly of white-skinned people is what creates Neighbor-Neverland.

The business owners had naively thought that if they were neighborly and ran an exceptional business, the business would be just that—business!

Neighbor-Neverland is the only place where you are not treated as a neighbor. And so these "neighbors" say: "I have no neighbors. I want no neighbors. You are not my neighbor. You are never my neighbor in Neighbor-Neverland!"

MIRROR-MIRROR (REFLECTING ALL)

THE MIRROR IS so important in our lives that one look isn't enough. The mirror serves well when there is a double take, a second look that goes beyond what is initially seen.

The mirror is a wonder to some, loved by some, disliked by others, but a source of reflection to all.

The "mirror-mirror on the wall" idea from the fairy tale is about reflecting double—both outside and inside.

Looking into the mirror, one person loves what they see; the other looks at the same image but dislikes what they see. Each hears what the other is thinking and relays that thought. "You love it," says the one who dislikes the image. "You dislike it," says the one who loves the image. They see the same thing but have opposing opinions regarding what they see.

Each observes the other person looking at a reflection of themselves and denying what they see. "I see that you see what I see, but you have a different opinion," each person says. As a result of their differing opinions, they declare, "You do not have the right to that opinion; it is in opposition to mine. Who do you think you are?" Yet most fail to see they are doing the very thing they object to others doing.

The conflict reflected in the exchange of what is liked and disliked is not seen by either person, though it is reflected to each. They say, "I can like or dislike based on [my reason], but you cannot do the same with [your reason]. The mirror reflects only what I see based upon my reason."

Often there are occasions when we look at the mirror and it reflects what we see, and we still don't like what is reflected. This is the reality that what is seen reflects the person. The reflection cannot change unless we make a change. Further, to change what is reflected, there must be a change in what affects the image being reflected.

In its simplicity, the mirror reflects what is. The mirror paradox is that what we see will not change until we change what we see.

The mirror is loved when reflecting the best of us, that which we want to be seen, yet disliked when showing the things on the outside we do not want to see, and even more so when it reflects the angry, ugly inside.

The mirror is especially disliked when it reflects failed attempts to cover up who we really are. Therefore, we think it is better or best when the mirror reflects how we see things, not how things really are. Regardless, though, no matter how hard we try, who we really are—the wart, the boil, the disfigurement—cannot be covered up. The mirror reflection reveals the attempted cover-up! Others see it (the angry, the ugly), but we don't.

The mirror is hated when reflecting the parts and pieces we want to hide but cannot. One person likes what they see; the other person does not. Neither says the other has the right to like or dislike what is seen. Instead, they say, "The mirror is reflecting something that I like or dislike. Look and see."

Consider your mirror can often be those around you, those with whom you have a relationship. In a marriage, you can look at your spouse and see a reflection of your relationship—happy or distant, warm or cold.

Our mirror is society, those around us.

The mirror reflects reality—what is seen—sometimes with the undesired effect of exposing what should remain hidden. If you see a wart on your face, you will do something about it so it is hidden, and if you could have prevented it, you would have done so.

The mirror serves its intended purpose by addressing unintended consequences. By seeing what is, though not wanted, like the wart on your face, it's possible to make changes based upon what is being reflected that otherwise would be unnoticed and in the end left unaddressed.

People often choose to deal with the mirror by ignoring it. Destroying the mirror is the answer to those who reject or dislike what they see or want to promote what they want to see. However, they destroy the mirror's purpose to their own peril. Destroying the mirror is the pathway to destroy self and society. It is impossible to destroy the mirror in life short of eliminating all life. Thus, the only way to rid oneself of the mirror is to simply not look into it—in other words, by ignoring it! A complex way we ignore is when we see things differently by redefining what is being reflected.

Ridding yourself and society of the mirror paves the way for acceptance of whatever is being presented, for by getting rid of the mirror, there is a complete disregard for what is reflected. The best way to advance what we like, desire, believe, hold fast to, and want to promote—regardless of any opinion, standard, or other determinants of a healthy society—is to ignore what is being reflected! Society is the mirror of likes and dislikes.

THE MIRROR REFLECTS THE MAJORITY BEING THE MINORITY

A mirror of history confirms that the numerical minority in a society typically likes what they see, while the majority tends to dislike what they see. The mirror reflects that the minority of people, those who like what they see, hold the majority of wealth and power. Conversely, the majority of people are minorities who have little wealth and power.

The mirror, even among those who like what they see, reflects that things are getting worse, not better. Those who like and accept what they see attribute the decline of society to the people who dislike what they see, thus rejecting things that others think are normal. "It is those minorities who are the problem," they might say.

Sometimes one looks at the mirror and dislikes what is reflected back or finds it embarrassing. Dislike can be ignored, but embarrassment usually provokes an action to make a correction. In this way, the mirror serves a great purpose, as there is often good that results from seeing the truth, or even embarrassment. The mirror, consistently accurate, reflects what cannot be denied or hidden from you. Its desire is for the greater good to be seen. The mirror reflects what you dislike, providing an opportunity to fix or change anything that is an embarrassment!

"KNOW SENSE"

We see things we don't like, and we see some things that we like and thus accept. Our world and our society reflect us, so the mirror reflects accurately. Some like and some dislike what they see, and even that is a needed reflection of society.

When reality is being reflected to us, we don't always like what we see. The mirror gives an accurate reflection to all, regardless of whether they like what they see. Society often dislikes the contrast in what is seen, saying in essence, "Can't we all just get along?"

The mirror reflects something one person likes and another person dislikes. For example, in the case of political parties, a third person could like or dislike both positions, saying, "I don't agree with either one of you!"

The mirror reflects reality without exception; it reflects preference, bias, and control. The mirror will reflect what it sees based on what you present it; what is reflects is based on *your* reality.

The mirror is a wonderful apparatus that is indispensable. The mirror is vital not just for the purpose of reflecting. What is seen brings the opportunity and hope to spur progress and success in life. You cannot know what you look like, what you are doing, what decisions to make, or the effects of those decisions if there is no mirror to show you the results of your decisions. To know, learn, and adjust, you must have an accurate picture.

The mirror has two principal aspects. First, the mirror reflects what is presented. Second, it does not differentiate between what is actual and what has been prepared to create a particular reflection.

The mirror reflects what is presented or what has been altered to receive the desired reflection. For example, we dress up before an interview to present the best image of ourselves. Some put on makeup before going on camera to control or cover up what is to be seen. While the mirror reflects accurately, what is seen is filtered through the person presenting the image. We often see only what others want us to see. We see in the mirror what has been prepared for us.

The mirror makes no judgment but provokes judgment.

The mirror is the common denominator, unable to alter or influence. It does not discriminate, distinguish, or decide how or what to reflect. The mirror gives no attention to the tainted perspective often influenced by experiences. It is not tied to any objective foundation or reality. It only reflects. The mirror does not reflect intent but reality.

We err by asking, "Can't we all just get along?" Alternatively, we err by looking at society without looking at ourselves.

It is good news that even when the presented image is painted over or altered, the mirror still reflects reality, whether you like it or not, accept it or reject it. The mirror cannot lie! We lie to ourselves by ignoring or redefining what is being reflected.

Rarely do we want to remember what was "before." Almost always, when looking at the mirror, when we're unable to pass without looking, we hope to see something pleasing, different, or better.

We usually want to look in the mirror only after the makeover, the do-over. Moreover, we consider that reasonable and acceptable. On the other hand, is it?

The mirror reflects accurately—without any comment, dialogue, or debate—what is physically seen. As the saying goes, "Beauty is in the eyes of the beholder." The mirror reflects what it sees, but the image is interpreted or filtered by the eyes, mind, experience, and standards of the one looking. As such, the mirror reflects *my* truth, not necessarily *the* truth, or even *a* truth. A reflection can look beautiful to one and ugly to another.

That which informs our perception is determined by *how* we see through our personal preferences, experiences, values, and tastes.

We each see reflections of specific, prepared presentations in the mirror. You dress up, put on makeup, and then look at your carefully manicured image in the mirror. What we see is most often a result of our own efforts. If what we see is not of our own making, the image is most often a result of outside influence. Therefore, *how* we see significantly influences *what* we see reflected to us in the mirror.

Most people will not say that what they see is of their own making; most will say they see the results of someone else's work. Society makes the same claim—what we see in society is not our doing but typically someone else's.

Long ago, it was said:

> The eye is the lamp of the body. If your eyes are healthy, your whole body will be full of light. Nevertheless, if your eyes are unhealthy, your whole body will be full of darkness. If then the light within you is darkness, how great is that darkness![1]

It is unhealthy to perceive what you see through the lens of, "It's rarely ever me; it's more likely them." When we process what we see in this manner, our entire life experience becomes a misrepresentation of reality.

Another ancient truth: "Remove the plank from your own eye instead of focusing on the speck in your brother's eye, and then you can see clearly."[2] Translated: what you see often is blurred by your own actions.

The mirror reflects the truth of how we perceive things with the eyes of our minds. One person sees the glass as half full while another sees it as half empty. The mirror reflects what we see and perceive in society. We must remember that the mirror has no care, no feelings; it has no opinions. It reflects only what is presented. The mirror's reflection is what it is! The mirror reflects the realities of the world as both the many and the one experience them.

Acceptance of what we see—the images projected back to us by the mirror—is often driven, dictated, and determined by society. It is shaped by those who influence the masses, those who are the most vocal or in power.

The mirror often reflects the thoughts, beliefs, and values of the loudest voices or those in power. The mirror accurately portrays what is internal by reflecting the external. The mirror is very much akin to an X-ray or MRI, which look beyond the exterior and into the interior, and then presents what it sees.

The mirror reflects the seen and the unseen!

MIRROR-MIRROR ABSURDITY

When the mirror shows something, the conclusion often is: it must be true and better for us, for surely the mirror would never reflect something negative or untrue. We must remember that the mirror reflects two realities: what really is and what we want to see. Often these realities are viewed through each person's perspective and are not necessarily what is best.

While the mirror reflects reality, it's the reality of what we want to see, not what is truly being reflected. Could this explain the countless overlooked, seemingly accepted, passive positions taken in society? Ignoring or redefining what is reflected diminishes the purpose of the mirror. History records crimes against groups of people and misuse of the mirror. When abused groups cried out, the mirror reflected those cries, albeit with attempts to show them to be normal or stifled, as no action was taken.

Over time, the mirror of society has a way of reflecting attempts to dismiss cover-ups, as well as impure motives, unjust laws, and misguided decisions. Overall, the mirror never fails to be true to itself, and if we look without discrimination, it will be faithful to those who look for the truth.

However, though it seems impossible, we control what we see reflected in the mirror. The mirror reflects truth, but that truth can only be seen devoid of personal bias; otherwise, it reflects the truth of a controlled reality.

Here is a conundrum: it is possible to damage the mirror to the point that the mirror itself alters what is reflected.

The mirror of society can be manipulated and preprogrammed and fail to accurately reflect truth. Instead, it has become a reflection of each person's truth or reality. We see what we want to see and term it the new reality or new norm.

No sense. Nonsense.

"Know Sense" would say, "The most effective way to change what you see is to deal with *how* you see."

Over the years, the mirror has accurately reflected how we see what we see. The shock of the past is no longer shocking. What was once outside the boundary or crossing the line is no longer. It is still shocking and crosses the line, but how we now see it has changed.

In the past, what we saw was taboo. To make the taboo acceptable, we had to first change how we perceive, ignore, or redefine the reflections of the mirror and have the mirror reflect the taboo so that it becomes what we want to see, rendering it no longer taboo.

If you cannot change what you see, change how you see what you see. In doing so, you change the apparatus. Everything we see is processed in this manner. If we successfully do this, we see it as reflecting the truth. This truth, though, is not *your* truth; it is perceived to be *the* truth.

The mirror's most significant and highest use is to reflect the truth, not what we want to see. Intuitively, we know this truth about the mirror and choose to manipulate its purpose or simply ignore it. If we could have our way, we would destroy the mirror, but we know we cannot. Frankly, we cannot do without the mirror.

The mirror achieves an even greater goal when it reflects and reveals what is not seen with the natural eye.

"I know what you see, but what do you perceive?" asks the mirror silently. The mirror seeks to pierce the exterior and reflect the interior.

The mirror, on its surface, shows only that which a person wants to be seen, that which makes one feel good about what is seen. But the true purpose of the mirror is to reach the realm beyond the natural eye.

Its reflection is based on what we do and who we are. The mirror's purpose is to show the truth so that, where needed, corrections can be made. Then we can feel good based not on how we see things but on how things truly are.

The mirror accurately reflects society and will continue to do so until we see the truth. What truth? The truth is that our society is broken. The truth is that we are not taking action to fix it. The truth is that our decisions and lack thereof contribute to our society's brokenness.

The mirror reflects the truth in our streets, communities, businesses, judicial system, places of worship, schools, families, and other relationships. The mirror reflects the reality experienced and what we want to see while simultaneously reflecting what is inside affecting, and at times infecting, the outside.

We cannot see the physical heart with our natural eyes. With the right tools, professionals can see the attributes that make up the heart. However, only the mirror can show us the intents of the heart—what is in the heart—by reflecting the actions of the heart that manifest as our thoughts, beliefs, and values. The mirror reflects the condition of the heart more accurately than a doctor or any imaging device ever could. It does so by reflecting the heart's condition through our society. The mirror reflects to us more than what the natural eyes can see and more than what we want and choose to see.

Being true to itself, the mirror desires for us to see reality and do something beneficial about what we see.

The quandary the mirror forces us to face is that one party can say he loves or likes what he sees and not have to feel or experience the frustration, upheaval, unrest, oppression, and even desperation in our society. Meanwhile, another party may dislike or hate the same thing someone else loves or likes. Both are reflected by the mirror. The mirror reflects the truth of our society.

Our world reflects who we are, and it is very telling.

There is a high probability that, if polled, most would agree that putting lipstick on a pig would make it look uglier. All would agree that it would look silly. The mirror has reflected that reality in our society and thus has served its purpose. Is the mirror possibly reflecting that we are living like pigs? Lipstick will not help!

One might say, "Mirror-Mirror, I don't like what I see. Am I angry at what I see, or am I angry at the mirror? If I cannot ignore, remove, or break the mirror, just don't force me to face it, as I don't want to see what I look like. I don't like what I see, as I don't want to see…reality."

Though we try to blame it, the problem is not the mirror.

24

YOU GOT ME GOING IN CIRCLES (THERE ARE NO POINTS IN A CIRCLE)

W E GIVE GREAT attention to what a person looks like yet little to their actions. We err in doing so, because what a person looks like truly matters as much as their actions. All too often people judge based on appearances to their detriment. When you make a judgment purely on what you see, you miss out. In doing so, you cause harm to those who never had an opportunity to be known. This pattern repeats itself, going in circles, around and around and around.

What you see is not always what you get. What you see with your eyes does not reflect who someone is. Often, even what you see about a person cannot reveal what that person thinks about himself or herself.

Try as I might, I labor to clothe myself to reflect who I am and how I think. Nevertheless, even those things are affected by internal conflict and external influences. Further, my mood and emotions contribute to how I present myself, and I often miss this mark, doing so based on the judgments people make without saying a word. I dress to impress but am never truly known.

In addition, while what you see may or may not be what you get, what you see can be very deceiving or "de-seeing"—you see only what

I want you to see. Alternatively, you see what you were expecting to see. However, none of it is reality. The reality has never been given a chance to be perceived. What's the point? Circles have no point.

One should judge not by the color of the skin but the content of the character, to paraphrase Dr. Martin Luther King Jr. Elsewhere it is written that man looks on the outside (to their detriment and undoing, exposing their weakness), but God looks at the heart![1] What is the distinction between the two? Regardless of one's position on God, why is looking merely at appearances an indication of our human flaws?

It was written long ago that it is not what goes into a man that makes him unclean but what comes out of him.[2] In other words, do not judge the container; consider what goes in or comes out of the container. That is the way to avoid going in circles.

The container is just that—the vessel. The size and shape can vary, but in and of itself, it is only a container. We fail when we make judgments based on the container. Perhaps the only proper judgment of a container is whether it reflects what it contains. This is not a circle but a significant point.

Looking only at what you see with your eyes is a killer of possibilities and progress. Looking with only your eyes blinds you from understanding what is beneath the surface. Seeing and knowing is not to be based on appearance but on experience!

Further, *what* you see with your eyes rarely tells *why* you see what you see. People present themselves a certain way by dressing up for a date or preparing a resume to be accepted, perhaps masking reality.

Alternatively, you see what you expected, not because it is what was presented but because it is what you desired to see. This happens to people in love. A person may not seem lovable, but they are loved because their spouse, boyfriend, or girlfriend desires to love them and has set an expectation to love them. No more circles, but a significant point has now been made.

Further, even *how* you see is very much shaped by your own biases, views, and experiences.

What is the best, most accurate judgment pattern for human beings? It is to base judgments on a person's conduct and character, not on what you see on the outside. That is just the container holding the truth of the person.

Labor and commit to block out life experiences and outside influences that inform *how* you see. No matter how good the container looks, dismiss the notion that it is a certain thing because it seems presidential, stately, official, grand, honorable, pious, or even holy. Don't judge the container. Avoid going in circles; give no regard to the container.

Avoid making judgments, taking action, or drawing conclusions based upon what you see with your eyes, hear with your ears, and even perceive with your mind. What *you* see, hear, and process does not consider others' perspectives, only yours. Their perspective often is different from yours because it is based on their experiences and understanding. This is a point, not a circle.

When you judge based on what you see, you do so to your own peril, for what is shown, crafted, and prepared by others is tainted, distorted, and not a true reflection of reality. This is a disruption of the pointless circle.

Relying upon your own, often myopic, understanding leads to drawing conclusions and even writing off someone because of how you perceive them, not because of who they are, what they do, or what they represent. You look at them on the surface—the container—and may consider their actions, but you never look beyond that. When that happens, the container is misjudged, accepted by some and rejected by others.

The actions of the container also cannot be judged solely based on external characteristics. Often what we see has been influenced by our actions or others' actions and not solely by those doing the act. They are acting perhaps out of force, having no other options.

The exit strategy from the circle is to cease judging and writing people off, as this is done to your detriment and demise.

Being dismissive of others and relying solely upon what you see with your eyes has proved again and again to be a giant mistake. It continues to be society's fatal flaw, the Achilles' heel. Yet history continues to repeat itself—and around we go in circles.

It is not those looking up to others whose vision is clouded, but those who look down on others. Those who have less tend to first consider how a person looks, then how they sound and what they say, and finally, what they promise and have done. Those who have less than others often misjudge, but they do so with an expectation based on need and the desire to have more.

The *haves* judge primarily based on who is or is not a threat to them. They care less about how a person looks but will prefer those who have something—money, power, position—and can look the part. The desired circle—you got me going in circles.

Judging based on character and conduct is the circle of life. Judging by appearances can result in death, hate, and division. It is an endless continuum—a circle without a point.

— 25 —

NOT ALWAYS–NEVER

A DISCERNING AND UNSUSPECTING passenger wrote:

Early one morning, I was riding to work on public transportation. I felt unsettled sitting next to a person with scars, bruises, and cuts on his face and arms. The train stopped in a historically poor community filled with dilapidated houses, and the person got off. As he did, I thought he was surely returning to a particular lifestyle, considering his environment. I even considered it while he was sitting next to me, which is why I was so unsettled and kept a close eye on him. I thought he may be up to no good and might do me harm.

Unable to nod off because I wanted to be alert and keep a watchful eye, I was happy and more at ease when he exited the train.

When I returned home after work that day, I was reminded of the stop and the person on the train. I looked out the window, and to my surprise, there was the same person. I saw him standing in front of a mother and her children, fighting to defend them from gang members.

I said two things to myself. First, *never* assume that a person's scars, bruises, and cuts mean they're up to no good because many times they have those scars as a result of others who were up to no good. They got them defending the poor and defenseless.

I was also reminded that our workplaces can be just as dangerous as some of the streets, causing scars, bruises, and cuts on people as they seek to defend the poor and defenseless.

I realized a greater truth: Never look at where a person works or has made their home and assume that means they are part of the problem. Many people have made their homes where the problems are so they can fix them!

--- 26 ---

THE PROBLEM

*M*an: Hey bro, I know I hear from God. He agrees with me all the time!

Woman: I know I hear from God. She always agrees with me!

Both: God and me, we got it going on—we agree on everything!

People often claim that God agrees with or supports their position on critical issues rather than conforming to His position. For those who honestly believe in God as Creator and Owner of all things, it's is a dangerous proposition.

--- 27 ---

YOUR WAY!

*I*t's my way or the highway" explains why there is so much gridlock on our freeways.

When we become stubbornly dogmatic, insisting on having things our way or else, we find ourselves alone. When it's my way or the highway, the highways become quickly gridlocked.

---- 28 ----

THE TRUE UP

*T*HE PACKAGE—PREFERRED BECAUSE of the outside, and what is inside leaves regrets.

The package—judged solely by the outside, and what is inside is never known.

*****

Most life experiences are filtered through our perceptions and processed by our mind guided by those perceptions. Both our perception and thought processes can be conditioned, influenced, or altered so our perception does not necessarily line up with our desires, reality, expectations, or true self.

The physical eye is complex. In a nanosecond, it can see and process almost limitless, simultaneous images and then capture and communicate them back to the brain.

As complex as the eye is, it renders things simple. In this simplicity, we perceive things, and oftentimes we do so lacking knowledge, understanding, discernment, and wisdom. We simply see things—and with mono-perception. We see one thing, often the one thing we *want* to see, filtered through and influenced by our biases, or how we have been conditioned to perceive the world around us.

We make judgments through the "simple" method of communicating perceptions after our mental processing.

We rarely allow room for our eyes to see beyond their limited ability. We rarely give our eyes a chance to get a second look, offering the hope or opportunity to inform our minds beyond what we have been influenced to believe. After our eyes deliver images, we rarely allow our minds to truly process the images to appreciate them. Instead, we judge.

One way to avoid the deception resulting from drawing conclusions based on what is seen by the eye and then processed by the mind is to test what is seen and processed.

Consider fruit. Once you see it, a piece of fruit passes the eye test. Once you smell it, it passes the sniff test. Then it must be tasted or experienced to determine whether what was seen and processed lines up with reality. It is one thing to say the apple looks good; it is another to know that the apple *is* good. What you experience must be "trued up"—it must be proved true when tested against what was seen or told. Otherwise, it is false!

To be true is to be "in accordance with the actual state or conditions; conforming to reality or fact; not false."[1] As the fruit example shows, the taste test is reality! The taste test is the "true up" of what the eye sees and the mind comprehends or perceives.

Consider the result if the fruit looked good, smelled good, and/or sounded good, but when tasted, was bitter and nasty, and no one wanted another bite. This is the taste test—the true up!

The "fruit"—the truth claim, the opinion, the belief—seemed great, felt good, and was said to be in our best interest, but when experienced, it did not line up with what we were told or expected. This is the taste test—the true up!

If you believe in right and wrong, good and evil, and truth, you are standing alone. If everyone and everything is against you, or seems to be against you, you have not yet fallen. They continue to complain, criticize, point fingers, and disappear on you, yet you still stand, though you are weary. This is the taste test—the true up!

If everyone else is on board and the majority is going in the same direction, it must be the right direction, right? Then something goes wrong, and what was said to be is not what is experienced. This is the taste test—the true up!

That taste test is wonderful but bittersweet, no matter what the fruit looks like or how good it smells. If it does not taste good, it does not pass the taste test.

The taste test is the true up.

Unblemished fruit looks good and is therefore perceived to be perfect, since nothing in its appearance seems unpleasing. However, often when bitten into, it is not good at all. The perfect-looking fruit is often bitter and disappointing and does not live up to its appearance. This is because there is a gap between appearance and reality.

Contrast the perfect fruit with one that is ugly and bruised, something we would view as undesirable. Such conditions—the bruises and imperfect appearance—often result from the fruit being ripe and ready to eat even though it doesn't appear so from the outside.

When fruit is ripe, it often falls to the ground, and that motion can bruise the fruit. Such fruit is not so appealing to the untrained eye. Such fruit needs not be trued up. In and of itself, it passes the taste test unchallenged. Yet it often fails to be tasted because it does not pass the eye and/or smell test, which can register false positives.

We often fail to enjoy the greatness life offers because we disregard the true up when it comes to our relationships with people. They may look a certain way, but have you gotten to know them? There may be a reason a person is bruised!

By now, you may realize that the bruised it is often sweeter. Take the taste test before making judgments!

29

STAND

WHICH IS THE most accurate statement: "If you do not stand for anything, you will fall for everything" or "If you are unwilling to fall for something, you will stand for anything?"

—— 30 ——

SCENE UNSEEN: THE SUBTLE UN-SCENE

Have you ever *scene*, or have you never *scene*?

The seen unseen scene is called denial. We want to believe something is not or should not be happening, so we do not acknowledge the scenes playing out before our eyes.

THE SUBTLE SCENE

There is no problem, argument, debate, or concern when white-colored people go to places such as Africa, the Caribbean, or Asia, or to areas that could be called underdeveloped or needy, and find themselves surrounded and being served by the locals. White-skinned people travel to these and other regions and are welcomed, entertained, and embraced with gladness, even integrating into their culture. Sharing secrets and invitations to homes and businesses almost always occur when white-skinned people visit these areas and regions.

THE NEVER SCENE

Rarely are dark-skinned people seen sitting while white-skinned people sing songs to them or escort them throughout their country with smiles of welcome and cameras flashing. If it does happen, it's not likely to be shown on a media outlet or the internet for all to view.

THE SEEN SCENE

Residents who know the history of their country are, in essence, subject-matter experts, and in certain regions of the world they are almost always people of color. They are also treated differently, even though they welcome all people with bright smiles and open arms.

Even if it is out of necessity because tourism is vital to their local economy, residents of color (who are often dark-skinned) serve, entertain, transport, and invite the white-skinned visitors to understand their culture. Almost always, they are accepting, and in some cases, they even invite them into their homes. It is so normal that most people don't notice it anymore; it is an expected part of the experience. Nothing abnormal is seen in these scenes; this is to be expected when visiting.

The Unseen Scene

Generally, we don't see white-skinned people welcoming dark-skinned visitors into their homes, and perhaps it is not even an expectation.

There are rarely large groups of white-skinned people singing to, dancing for, or sharing their culture with dark-skinned people. A white-skinned person sharing the local food, natural landscape, and cultural history with a dark-skinned person to communicate their pride in their culture is almost unheard of anywhere in the world. It's the unseen scene.

We don't see white-skinned people telling dark-skinned people, "We are happy you are here" in the same manner. They are, perhaps, happy to have visitors but not happy that those visitors are dark-skinned. The subtle difference is "un-scene."

The Subtle Un-Scene

Perhaps this is so, at least partly, because the way white-skinned people have treated others historically is not so complimentary to their culture.

Again, the unseen scene is that there are few productions in which a person who is dark-skinned is being entertained, surrounded, or served by someone who is white-skinned.

It is hard to locate productions showing a dark-skinned person or couple traveling through a country, stopping off here and there, and being welcomed, hosted, entertained, and served by white-skinned people in the same way we see dark-skinned people doing in Africa, the Caribbean, or other parts of the world. There are exceptions, but very few scenes show white-colored people happily welcoming, assisting, and serving darker-skinned people.

UNSEEN SCENES

With things remaining the same, it is unlikely that we will ever see a sitcom or drama that shows a white-skinned person serving or entertaining a dark-skinned person.

THE SUBTLE SCENES SEEN

The experiences we see in the theater of life are assumed to be normal, with the reality of the impact suppressed, downplayed, or ignored. If the reality of their impact is ever broached, if a challenge is issued, it is done softly, apologetically. Most scenes are produced through the skewed lenses of those producing them, reflecting their reality and not society's overall or the reality of those most affected.

In films from years ago, dark-colored people were hardly even allowed on the scene. They were the firsts in the rare scenes they appeared in: the first to die, the first to be sacrificed, the first to be bought into servitude, the first to be ridiculed. These were the subtle and perhaps not-so-subtle seen scenes. Whether this was coincidental or intentional depends on who you ask.

SCENES SEEN

Thankfully, the realities of our world are not being shown in productions of fiction, which is OK. What's not OK is that the nonfictional realities, such as those seen in the movie *Hidden Figures* (and many others "hidden") are being suppressed, with a few released only when producers are forced or compelled or it is convenient.

THE NOT-SO-SUBTLE SCENES SEEN

There are exceptions, of course. However, even the exceptions are scenes seen to feel good. It is expected for these scenes to be overlooked. One worth noting is *The Blind Side*, a film based on a true story that showcases a white couple's choice to do the right human thing for a dark-skinned person.

THE SUBTLE SEEN SCENE

As great as this true story is, the irony is it is most remembered for what the white family did for the dark-skinned person. So often, the narrative focuses on what a white-skinned person does for a dark-colored person, and it should be applauded when a *have* does something for a *have-not*. Progress will be made when a story is promoted and applauded that tells of a dark-skinned person who does something for a white-skinned person.

THE SUBTLE, NEVER-SEEN SCENES

There are examples. Of note are films featuring actor Sidney Poitier. He was cast mainly in movies where his character challenged society and/or white-skinned people. These films pushed the envelope and broke barriers in unprecedented ways.

Poitier's characters would confront the system and almost always survive obstacles, oppression, hate, denial, death threats, inhumane treatment, and racial slurs, which represented the short list of realities faced by dark-skinned people. The characters he portrayed would have to outwit, survive, or endure covert and overt discrimination based solely on skin color. He did so with the highest of character.

THE SCENES SEEN NEVER SEEN

The message in Sidney Poitier's movies was almost always that dark-skinned people were not less than white-skinned people. But sadly, such scenes are largely unseen in this age, and what remains to be seen is a reminder of the need for those scenes to be reality.

THE SUBTLE NEVER SEEN—WILL IT EVER BE SCENE?

It will be difficult, if not impossible, to see an honest portrayal in fiction when there is no picture to draw from in nonfiction. To see and accept those scenes on the screen and for them to be realistic, we must first see them in our reality, our streets, and our lives.

31

YOU SCARE ME!

I HAD A DREAM that scared me.

I saw myself walking with my wife in one of our city's downtown urban areas, where mainly minorities and the homeless live. In this part of town, people live in tents and under viaducts, push shopping carts filled with all their worldly belongings, and sleep wherever they can find a "safe," restful spot. Because my wife and I were looking to be good, sensitive, and neighborly, we wanted to be a blessing to a homeless person.

We wanted to help, but we also felt uneasy about helping these individuals who could not help themselves. Although we grew up in what many would characterize as a poor and perhaps dangerous neighborhood, we now lived far away, in the suburbs. However, that did not mean we were not mindful of where we came from, and we wanted to give back.

As we walked, I could not shake an uneasy feeling, and then I realized I was sensing a touch of fear.

We were trying to do well and be a blessing to someone else, yet we were on guard. We were afraid even while trying to be a blessing.

What bothered me most was that even I had a sense of fear. I reflected on where I grew up. Bad guys terrorized our neighborhood, while most others in the neighborhood were just struggling to live.

While my wife and I wanted to make an impact, we were afraid of the very people we wanted to touch.

"Why?" I pondered. Was it because the others did not look or act in a manner our minds could process or accept? Was it their clothing or perhaps their lack of cleanliness that caused the uneasiness? We wanted to be a blessing but were afraid of the very people we wanted to help.

To our shock, as we approached a person with a few dollars in our hands, the man, clearly homeless, was afraid of us too. We did not realize fully at the time that he saw us as people who might harm him.

In our desire to be a blessing, we walked toward the homeless person, keeping a respectful distance while holding our hands out, making sure he saw the money. We walked for a few blocks. The faster we walked, the faster he walked, and we gave up trying to give. There was sadness on his face as he fled but also relief, as the brief encounter had caused more fear for him.

"What just happened?" we asked. We wondered if perhaps the homeless man feared us more than we feared him. Then we further pondered that maybe he had more reason to fear us than we had to fear him.

Admittedly, our fear was primarily founded on his appearance. His fear may also have been based on our appearance. I could imagine him saying, "It is those people who have done harm to me."

The reality of what happened was that a need went unmet because both parties feared each other. I thought that perhaps one precursor to becoming homeless is when a need or needs are unmet. Is it possible that our fear of one another is what creates and perpetuates homelessness within our communities?

I thought about the many times when I could have given financially to help the homeless but did not, thinking the person might be taking advantage of me. I've been told that some people make a living standing on the streets holding signs that say, "Homeless. Need help. God bless." I considered that meeting the need could be seen as enablement. I know giving to certain people does them more harm than good.

Both parties feared each other. Then, added to the equation, was not wanting to waste what I was giving by being taken advantage of. I was also reminded that it has been said, "The poor you will always have with you."[1] Therefore, I resolved to set my mind at ease and accept that I cannot give to everyone.

Yet even with this practical realization, I was reminded that there remained large populations with unmet needs. The attempt to meet the need was unsuccessful, the effort being negated by fear and pragmatism.

Perhaps the most effective way to cancel the effects of fear in this exchange is by simply being compassionate. True compassion is willing to give sacrificially, even if it means being taken advantage of in the process. While it may not be appreciated by all, it is appreciated by some.

Compassion reminds us "it is more blessed to give than to receive."[2]

When the giver fears the homeless and the homeless fear the giver, the blessings intended for both are canceled. One cannot give, and the other cannot receive!

What scared me most about my dream was that it was not a dream.

—————————— 32 ——————————

PROGRESS, CHANGE, AND ADVANCEMENT

PROGRESS AND ADVANCEMENT require *change*.
Meaningful change that leads to progress and advancement is beneficial. Progress and advancement provide change that brings something better than what existed before. Acceptable change mirroring progress and advancement must be validated by self-evident accountability through universal societal experience. The test of effectiveness discounts those who promote change for their specific benefit or agenda, or as a matter of choice.

Change tested: Many things in our world make no sense, as they have proven themselves to be nonsense, not by opinion but by evidence. There are two major points. First, a thing cannot stand the test of time if it is unsustainable, and second, the changes made have led to a degrading of our society. Regarding the second point, the test reveals that if you have money, you are insulated and isolated as a result of having.

As a society, the test we are to rely upon is the overall, universal experience and impact of changes. The universal test asks, "Are we all better off today than we were yesterday?" This is not based on the experience of one or a few, but on the many realizing that some things will never bring progress and advancement!

Progress and advancement defined: The terms *progress* and *advancement* should not be used based on convenience or opportunism. Frequent change is not in itself progress and advancement. Evolution—change over time—does not automatically mean things have improved. When defining progress and advancement, we should ask if the change has made the world safer and more peaceful, and created opportunities for all.

A thriving society is built on a foundation of progress and advancement. Therefore, progress and advancement must be embraced, promoted, and pursued.

Progress and advancement hitting the mark: Progress and advancement should be just that: progress and advancement. This is to say it should move our society from what was thought to be the target to the actual target. A trip to the moon requires constant adjustments or changes for the spacecraft to reach its target. Adjustments and changes can hit *a* target, but it can only be successful when it hits the intended target. The target is progress and advancement. With the adjustments and changes, it should be clearly seen without asking if there has been progress and advancement.

We can know real progress and advancement when it is affirmed through the eyes and voices of the many. Perhaps the greatest evidence of progress and advancement is when those who are least or last to be touched by progress and advancement agree that it is happening.

Progress and advancement tested: Progress and advancement should not happen by redefining it to fit new ways of thinking or so-called progressive thinking. Calling something progressive does not make it so. A good though simplistic test would be to ask if the progress has brought peace. Is there peace among all people throughout the land? Of course, we must first consider whether peace for all is even possible to attain.

Peace extinguishes or replaces fear and is experienced when people feel safe. We are often robbed of peace and live in fear as a result of opportunities being denied or stolen.

Opportunity is the pathway to peace and safety. It could be said that when you are busy being who you are, with no oppression or obstacles standing in your way, you are at peace.

Progress and advancement proven to be failing: With technology leading the way, we can say our so-called evolution has not been beneficial. Thus, we have little to no peace. Opportunities abound but not to all. There are more opportunities for the few than for the many. The few may proclaim progress and advancement, but not the many.

Progress and advancement camouflaged: We can do many things based on our learning and discoveries. In the name of progress, we have used rotary phones, vinyl albums, printed photos, books, and newspapers. These were all used in years past to make life easier and more convenient for us as a society.

Specific advancements in our society, such as access to information through the internet, have helped us become more connected and improve our quality of life.

Progress and advancement endangered: Being more informed is the key to progress and advancement, as we assume the more we learn, the better we will be. In the past, if a person was better informed, they would help more, serve more, and even give more. Overall, it would be said that the person evolved into a productive citizen.

The progress was proven, as evolution was tied to being neighbor-focused instead of self-focused. This does not suggest that anyone would disregard their personal obligations to their own family but that they would look out for their neighbor too.

For progress and evolution to occur, society would need to benefit from the new information learned.

We are now shelving the past in the name of progress, advancement, and evolving, just to say we are moving forward. We say, "We must evolve, we are evolving, and evolution is a byproduct or evidence of progress and advancement." We say in the name of being progressive that things must change regardless of the impact on society.

Inept changes: For there to be progress and advancement, there must be change, and change must reflect progress and advancement; otherwise, it is neither. Something that is neither progress nor advancement is something that changes for the sake of changing or that changes for the worse.

Change tested and failed: Change for the sake of change is what we now call evolution or progressive thinking. We think, "As long as we are changing—shelving the old and bringing in the new—we are evolving and are better off!"

Most often, only a minority of people claim that change for the sake of change is evolution. Yet we all experience effects of change because we are forced to do so in the name of acceptance and being progressive.

However, the voices that speak loudest because they have a platform do not necessarily speak best, speak truth, or say what is representative of the masses' way of thinking. There are many who say they are the voice of the people. Some are; others are not. Many of these voices promote only themselves, their group, or their agenda.

We have been told that anything that does not embrace change is archaic, backward, ignorant, and the same as discrimination and hate. These voices have been the minority, and the evolution underway has been specific to their agenda, perspective, needs, and desires. Their ambitions have been applauded in the name of change. They ask, "What society would ever want to stay the same, not evolve, and not change?"

Change tested: It is unreasonable for a society, or even one person, to think one can truly arrive and avoid self-evaluation by proclaiming themselves to have evolved and progressed and labeling those who disagree with their progressive and evolved thinking as ignorant. Such a position is taken to one's own detriment.

Progressive thinking needs change: It is not the thing that needs to change but how you view or deal with the thing. Progress could be seen in simple changes, such as going from knowing how something was done in the past to understanding why something was done that way.

A statement of understanding regarding change of progressive thinking: Progressive thinking demands acceptance and agreement but does not offer or embrace the same.

Progressive thinking rejects real change: Real change should be to say, "I understand the premise back then, and it seemed to make sense but did not work as desired, and now this change will work as originally intended or desired." Real change's intentions must be tried and tested, and the results must prove to bring progress and advancement.

Progress and advancement unchanged: Most people prefer things to remain the same, and at times that is best. We find most often that minorities are change agents. It is the minority groups who feel negative or unintended consequences of the lack of change and, therefore, are more motivated toward change.

The value of progress and change: Progress is indeed made when the minority has a voice and that voice is not stifled, minimized, dismissed, ignored, or made to seem unimportant or irrelevant. The real test of progress is whether the minority voice is valued.

To value someone is to consider what is being spoken or stated. What is their point of view? If their perspective is not understood, at least it can be heard. Those who champion progress and evolution seek to know how it would feel to be treated like the minority but use their own standards.

Abuse of evolution, progress, and change: We will know that we have evolved when the majority in power makes decisions that favor the minority.

Evolution misuse: One known attribute of the majority is one's standing at birth. They say, "We can all think, so we should all be heard." While this standard makes clear sense, it also has been misused and abused, and now what it means to be progressive and evolved makes no sense.

Minorities are defined by what is seen, as in the color of their skin. Actions, conduct, and character matter also but only to a minority of observers. Values, beliefs, and convictions support positions and should not be dismissed solely because they are in the minority.

Progress and advancement—the voice that needs no change: Some say the minority voice that is contrary to change for the sake of change or that does not support the idea that evolution and progressive thinking are always progressive is the voice that needs no change. However, the voice that needs no change is not the loudest or most popular.

Progress and advancement clarified: The voice that needs no change does not speak, nor does it seek or promote choice. Instead, it defends non-choice as the differentiator. The voice of reason and sense says, even if in the minority, "This makes no sense and is nonsense."

The minority voice that needs no change would say, "Not inviting anyone and everyone is not evidence of ignorance or a lack of progression." They would say, "Inclusion and diversity are accurately applied to those who have no choice in the matter."

The voice of advancement and progress that needs no change warns us to be careful of those who would offer their choices as equal to that of those who have no choice. The voice that needs no change would remind us that sex offenders, pedophiles, and even gangsters could say, "I was born this way; I cannot help myself." There are still others who would say, "This is just the way I feel." Both would ask, "Why shouldn't I be invited to the table?"

The voice that needs no change would remind us that if a person's choice makes them a minority, they cannot equate their experience with that of those who are minorities without choosing to be so.

Progressive thinking unchecked: The new minorities at the table are those who will say, "Everyone should be at the table except those who would prevent everyone from being at the table." They say anyone and everyone should be at the table where No Sense and Nonsense converge. And yet, Know Sense, being in the minority, is not invited.

Progress, advancement, and evolution forced: We are at a place and time that rationalizes everything in the name of evolution and progressive thinking. We say we have evolved with such rationalization in the name of diversity, inclusion, acceptance, tolerance, evolution, progress, and higher thinking.

Progress and advancement Know Sense: At this point, sense, or Know Sense, which is in the minority, must prove itself to have some degree of influential knowledge.

Two weapons are used to try to defeat *Know Sense*, or common sense, which cannot be defeated. The first is to speak over the voice of sense to cancel it or create confusion. It is hoped that the loudest voice gets attention and is worthy of being heard and its message is considered truth. The second weapon is to generalize anything or anyone that does not agree with progressive thinking and put them in an opposing category. This weapon promotes the idea that anyone who is against a particular definition of evolution—the changes in our society that redefine what once was standard, suggesting that there is a plumb line—is ignorant, uninformed, biased, bigoted, and even racist.

Progress and advancement changed: Know Sense protects and defends those who have no choice, people born as they are, each male or female, but tagged as ignorant and uninformed. Know Sense is even said not to be progressive when it defends those who have no choice from those who try to set new standards by redefining terms to accommodate those who have a choice.

Progress advancement changes Know Sense: Sense is founded upon what is known and what a person can sense. They say, "This is what I know based on what I can sense. Where it makes sense, I know peace; where it does not make sense, I sense no peace."

Know Sense, while in the minority, is uncommon and considered nonsense or *no sense*. However, being in the minority does not mean that one is wrong, outdated, obsolete, or nonsense.

We once sensed truth based upon reality, but now we ignore what we see and experience. We block our senses, and over time they become seared to the point that we have no feelings and cannot sense anything. This also results in us dismissing the unintended consequences and convincing ourselves that what we sense, see, or experience is not reality. We know we are not at peace, but we are unwilling to accept our choices as being a result of or affected by a lack of peace.

What is happening in our society, world, and lives is not a result of our choices. We are told that evolution and progressive thinking are the only things that matter. Gender-neutral bathrooms, a man suddenly feeling like a woman, video games that disrespect women, programming that portrays meaningless killing—evolution and progressive thinking says there are no natural consequences. This is the redefining of sense.

The voice that should be heard is that of a minority group who has made a choice that they have no choice but to stay with sense. They ask, "Why am I not accepted for rejecting and hating things I disagree with, things that do not fit tested sense? I was born this way—to *know sense*—and even if you disagree, this is how I feel. I do not agree with the majority, and sometimes I don't even agree with the minority. The only thing that matters is that I can be who I am. If in being true to myself I choose to be who I am, why do you reject me? Why are you, progressive thinkers, not inviting me to the table, as progressive as you are?"

Progress and advancement: Our society has evolved and progressed to the point that it accepts everything but rejects those not accepting of its perspective.

Progressive thinking says, "Those who reject what is new and different are non-progressive, as we progressives accept all newcomers! We reject the old, and we reject the new at our discretion. This answers the question, "Why do you not accept me?" The answer is that they don't accept everything! Evolution and progressive thinking only accepts that which fits its agenda and is convenient for its cause.

Contrary to progress and evolution, Know Sense proves itself to be true, as there is a time, place, position, situation, and scenario when one should *not* be accepted.

Acceptance on trial—Know Sense versus evolution and progressive thinking: Know Sense accepts anyone who has no choice but is born or created that way. The criterion fits all and never changes.

Evolution and progressive thinking accept anything and anyone based on how they feel, how they profess to have been born, and even how others, representing the most popular and most prevalent views, perceive them.

The voice of Know Sense is almost always the minority. All too often, evolution and progressive thinking are the majority voices. We must be reminded that the loudest voices do not necessarily represent what is true, best, or desired.

There is a voice that says, "I don't like a certain group of people, and because my views are not accepted, my voice is not allowed in the conversation, and I am not invited to the table." Yet another voice says, "You say, 'We all should be all-inclusive.' With this being so, shouldn't I be included in the discussion in the name of diversity? Instead of being diverse and inclusive, you are actually being intolerant."

Because I disagree with or don't accept a particular group, you tag me as intolerant and do not invite me to the table even though I am different.

Know Sense joins No Sense: It is said that in the name of progressive thinking, we must add beneficial diversity; otherwise, we are not being inclusive. Let Know Sense have a voice too, and you might begin to *know sense* in the name of "progress < change > advancement."

— 33 —

WHAT'S THE MATTER?

I DON'T CARE; NOTHING matters." While this is not said aloud, it is almost always lived.

"Do not move an ancient boundary stone."[1]

There are things that matter and should matter; however, we live in a day, age, and time when almost nothing matters. The operative word is matter. The argument or debate is what is matter or substance. Matter could be tied to consequence, but for now, in this conversation, it is simply a matter of substance or importance.

Raising kids with a male and female in the home used to matter.

Taking care of your mom and dad as they age used to matter.

A mother sacrificing herself to have the privilege and enjoyment of nurturing her child used to matter.

Owning content you could touch, store, catalog, and perhaps showcase used to matter.

Owning something versus renting or streaming used to matter.

Paying as you go and buying what you can afford versus borrowing and going into debt used to matter.

Ancient boundaries that once mattered not only have been challenged (as they should be to gain understanding); they are now breached without understanding. And lacking understanding and disregarding the consequences, those boundaries are ignored.

We say something is outdated, obsolete, not progressive, or ignorant. We think, "If the old does not agree with or fit with the new, the problem is the old, not the new." Remove the ancient, outdated, obsolete, non-progressive boundary.

Individual, societal, and governmental decisions used to matter. But in our march toward having things our own way, we disregard and dismiss consequences, as we say our decisions themselves do not matter.

The only matter that matters is how we feel at the time we make the decision. And then we ask, "What's the matter?"

CLARITY VS. CONFUSION

Cracking the Confusion Code

In a world of open access to communication, it is often impossible to distinguish truth from lie, real from unreal, or reality from fiction. Anyone with access to social media can broadcast misinformation to a global audience and within seconds create conflict or confusion.

There are now multitudes of voices competing for our time, attention, votes, support, and money. Who we decide to listen to helps determine how successful we will be in the end, so we have to choose carefully.

In this section, we will identify some of the most common offenders, as well as discuss how to crack the code of confusion and achieve and maintain a clear mind.

— **34** —

CHOICE: NOT FOR SALE

M AKE YOUR CHOICE before others make it for you.
Choice—it may be part of evolutionary theory, but it is not part of the university of diversity.

In the name of enlightenment and being progressive, it has been said that we have evolved to the point that leaving anything or anyone out is an act of judgment, prejudice, racism, bigotry, and sheer intolerance.

Anti-progressive, backward, antiquated, and ignorant are just a few of the labels given to any belief system that does not embrace the new progressive thinking we are forced to grapple with from media outlets, publications, and other sources. If you accept it, you are tagged as being non-progressive, and any lack of acceptance is considered ignorance.

The progressive world we now live in allows the view that someone can be born one way but after birth, change their gender, ethnicity, or other factors by choice, usually because of how they feel or what they believe about themselves.

Some would argue that they did not have a choice about whether to make this change and that they were simply born in the wrong body. Someone might say, "I see one thing in the mirror, but I know how I feel. I was born the wrong way, so I am compelled to change, not by choice but by my reality."

However, the reality is that when one is born one way and feels another way—regardless of influence, experience, or belief—they can still choose to accept or reject those feelings. How we feel is not always reality, and feelings change over time.

In our new, progressive world, people can still make choices, and those choices matter. What we believe in and live by, which way we go, what we choose, what we do—these are all choices we can still make.

It is a popular theme today to live based on how we feel. We all are free to make choices based on our feelings, and we often do. However, we must be careful not to draw conclusions or establish standards based upon choices guided by feelings because we have a choice in this too.

Choices based on feelings or popular views, errant as they may be, are considered enlightened and progressive. "We have evolved!" is the claim by progressives, and they say we need to adjust our views accordingly.

It is commonly held that those who make such choices should be leading conversations about inclusion and diversity because they are progressive. With this thinking, anyone and everyone should be invited and accepted into any and all conversations in the spirit of inclusion.

Suppose making choices based on how one feels is progressive. That would mean those who hold this view should become leaders for conversations about inclusivity and diversity. It means the person who approves of something should be at the table with the person who disapproves. Considering this, there should be no argument, debate, or challenge; after all, that is progressive and inclusive.

The thinking is that there is no right or wrong, good or bad, as the only way to be inclusive is to rid society and ourselves of absolutes.

The first major absolute to eliminate is choice. The needle is pushed, and terms are redefined according to whatever is convenient and popular. The reality is minimized by claims that people are born a certain way and have no choice in whether to change. Someone can easily say, "I have no choice in the matter!"

Inclusion and diversity accept and promote those who say they have "changed" but had no choice about who they truly were. Meanwhile, others have said they changed by choice, based on their feelings.

The easiest path—the expressway to a free pass in acceptance of inclusion—is to proclaim that one has no choice.

Choice, therefore, should be added to the discussion of inclusion by proclaiming that a choice cannot be made wrongly when based solely on feelings. Progressive reasoning demands that inclusion not care about the choice made.

Such thinking would allow followers of groups now viewed as hate groups to rightly say exclusion means not being inclusive. They could say, "We did not choose this ideology. We were born into an environment that shaped us into who we were. We had no choice in the matter. People do not make choices—choices are made for them."

If choices are made for us and we have no say in the matter, everyone should be welcomed to the table in the name of inclusivity, equity, diversity, and belonging, because they did not choose their way of thinking. Either it was forced upon them or they were born that way.

If groups now viewed as hate groups are not invited to the table, the standards of inclusivity would be violated because everyone is supposed to be given an equal voice. Thus, those excluded could argue, "I am not accepted; I have been set aside by society. You don't like me, but I was born this way! I had no choice in the matter."

There are two realities in this regard: those born with a certain skin color had no choice in the matter, and those who say they were born in the wrong body—they too had no choice in the matter.

Progressive thinking has determined that both should be viewed the same way. Proponents say that to be inclusive and diverse, one should make no distinction between a person's identity, ideology, and beliefs. Yet progressives themselves make distinctions that are not inclusive.

Progressive thinking does not include anything or anyone that does not agree with it. When something or someone does not agree with progressive thinking, it is termed ignorant or non-progressive.

One of the greatest attributes that sets humanity apart from all other creatures is free will, the ability to choose. Free will affords choice, which we can make with or without feelings.

All creatures except humans are controlled by their basic instincts. They have no choice in how they act. Put almost any food before a pig or a dog, and it will eat it. A vulture will never pass a meal that is not moving, the more rotten the better. If you inadvertently encroach the territory of a bear or a lion, regardless of intent, you will rouse their protective instincts, possibly to your own peril. You may find two same-sex animals snoozing, and some have even engaged in mating, but reproduction cannot occur.

If every creature was made to engage in same-sex relationships, there could be no reproduction, and the animal kingdom as we know it would fail to exist. This is why in animal sanctuaries, zoos, and the like, whenever there is the need to avoid extinction, the first step is to put males and females together. The animals engage by instinct more than by choice.

Animals don't choose their actions; they are not self-aware. When animals attack, it could be said they cannot help themselves and are just doing what comes naturally, following their basic instincts.

Humans may say, "I could not help myself." Nevertheless, we can choose, even if our choices are driven by certain influences or instincts. Humans can resist if they desire to do so. Alternatively, they can succumb to urges.

Animals live with no conscience and care little for the consequences of their actions. While they can feel physical pain, they have no emotions to hurt. In addition, they have no feelings when they hurt you.

All human beings are born with the ability to make choices. Though some may argue that choices have been made for them and they have limited options, we all always have choices.

When given no choice, it becomes a choice of consequence or conscience. If you refuse to participate in a prearranged marriage, what is the consequence? If you are drafted into the military and refuse to fight, what is the consequence? Put rotten food before a starving person, and they will have to choose to eat. In all these situations, we have a choice in the matter.

If we believe we have no choice in the matter, we could still be told, "Do this or die." However, even in that, we still have a choice. We can choose our own demise and die.

The great challenge brought on by progressive thinking is that those who disagree with their thinking are tagged as hate-filled, ignorant, and single-minded. Do not all humans have the same right of choice? Yes! Then why does progressive thinking look to deny another's right to choose differently? Why are those who choose a different path excluded from the inclusion and diversity party? It seems as if choice is not welcome at this party.

Progressive reasoning fails the "I had no choice" test. It looks into the mirror and realizes what it sees but says, "That's not how I feel! I choose to reject what I see and change because what I see does not line up with how I feel, what I believe, and even what I've been told." Progressive thinking fails the choice test because it does not align ideas with empirical truth. It says, "I know how I feel [thoughts and beliefs], but I know what I see [reality and consequences]!"

Beware and be aware when choice is attached to inclusivity and defined as progress, evolved, or higher thinking. Such choice tends to masquerade as diversity, but the resulting reality is that the choice leads to deconstruction and, ultimately, destruction.

Progressives say inclusion and diversity are best on display when choice is absent.

We should not be likened to animals, which have no choice. If we choose to change our original design, we should not rename it but rather *own* it. After all, it is *your* choice—*a choice you made.* Own it, as it is your choice and no one else's, so don't peddle it.

35

PLUMB LINE

W E CAN ALL be *wrong*, but we cannot all be *right*.
While some people like having fifty shades of gray, when it comes to life principles, the problem in our society is that there are too many shades of truth. Blending colors to make a new one is wonderful when painting a mural, but it is not a sustainable formula for decision-making.

In fact, history shows that this *and* that is not better than but in conflict with this *or* that. While to some degree we innately resist choosing one or the other as objective truth, we are prone to accept subjective truth by accepting or integrating this and that. We think, "My options should not be limited; the more options to integrate the merrier!"

However, as much as we love integrating options, we also realize the need for a reference point. People long for anchors that produce definitive and predictable outcomes.

How uncomfortable people become when given only two options, either this or that. They say, "Why can't there be alternatives? Options? Why do things have to be either right or wrong, black or white, true or false? Why can't there be something in the middle? How come it can't be this *and* that rather than this *or* that? Why can't how I see it be the right way? Why limit it to black or white when there are thousands of colors? Why must we be limited to true and false when the answer can be, "It depends"? Why must I be forced into a box of good or bad? Why can't something be good if it's good for me and bad if it's bad for me, regardless of what others say? Why does life have to be filled with either-or scenarios?"

Either-or. What could *or* mean? It could be an acronym for the operating room. It's also a conjunction "used to connect words, phrases, or clauses representing alternatives: books or magazines, to be or not to be."[1]

We find that there are only a few options. Anything offered can be added to, changed in the operating room, or resolved to be one or the other. There is a natural dislike of either-or, so we typically gravitate to changing, modifying, or at minimum, rejecting what is offered.

With the reality of our desire to have options, we still realize that a plumb line or reference point is necessary to aid us in navigating where we ultimately desire to arrive.

We all look for the point of truth that satisfies our self-worth. We desire to attain without forcing it, saying, "It will be simply because I want it to be." Having your way does not equate to realizing that what you desire is best. We may get what we want but find that it is not what we wanted.

This *or* that has always proven to be better than this *and* that!

Good is good. Bad is bad. Right is right. Wrong is wrong. Black is black. White is white. True is true. In addition, false is false. There's nothing left to the imagination or interpretation. We can all be wrong, but we cannot all be right. There must be a right after everything is proven wrong. The great news with this or that is that you get to reject or accept.

Nevertheless, you may ask, "Who gets to determine right or wrong? What makes your perspective or position better than mine, or what makes my perspective better than yours? Why can't what is right for me be right and what is right for you also be right? What makes me wrong and you right? What makes me right and you wrong? Who am I, and who are you? What qualifies you or me?

When there is no right or wrong, whatever is right for you can be right for you while simultaneously wrong for me. Moreover, it multiplies when others are added. Someone may agree with you, but others may not, so it goes on and on. We all have different viewpoints, as if there is no right or wrong. Anarchy typically follows when there is no right or wrong, no absolute truth.

There has to be a plumb line for there to be any meaning and progress. While subject to debate, criticism, and challenge, the plumb line must be self-defensible, unaided, unimpeded, and able to stand in and of itself. After all, it is the plumb line.

The biases and agendas of those who have strong convictions or are driven by their own desires and want their worldview to be everyone's worldview cannot have a say in the plumb line. Such voices change, as they are based upon feelings and experiences, and deny any objective standard.

A plumb line must be identified and used as the standard.

Various opinions, experiences, and beliefs lead people to land at a place where they will say, "I am right," with the hope of getting others to support them. The problem with standing alone is that you are standing alone. It is hard to argue the point when you have no followers.

Truth is unassailable.

A plumb line. Who needs it? Everyone!

---- 36 ----

THE DUMMY AND THE VENTRILOQUIST

THERE IS A perversion between the *created* and *Creator*. Imagine a mind driven mad and a conversation gone bad ...

Dummy: Who are you talking to?

Ventriloquist: Who are *you* to talk back to me? You would be nothing if you did not have me to express yourself.

Dummy: Who are you to say that to me? You'd better shut up.

Ventriloquist: Who do you think you are? You would not exist and could not talk if I did not give you a voice. You would be only a dumb, lifeless thing with no purpose if I hadn't given you a life. And that is your only purpose, to serve me as I see fit! In addition, I see fit to entertain others at my will. As you have no will because you are not alive, I wonder why I am even speaking to you. What has happened to me?

Dummy: You may give me my voice, but I have given you the means to express yourself.

Ventriloquist: Who are you talking to? You don't own me. I own you and can do whatever I choose, so I will tell you what has happened to you since you have not figured out that you are not in control. I control you. Without me, you are nothing. Without me, you would not have a voice, a platform. I use you as a second expression of myself. I am as necessary as you are—actually more, as without me, you are lifeless. You have no purpose, no future, no direction, no meaning, and I still struggle to figure out why I even put up with you!

Dummy: Were it not for me, you would not have a voice. You could not express yourself. Without me, you are lifeless.

This conversation takes place only when one confused voice speaks from a disturbed mind that is unable to distinguish the created from the Creator.

37

WHAT IS TRUTH? (NO DEFENSE)

WHAT IF THERE is *one truth*—not "a" truth, but "the" *truth*?

It's often said, "The older generation, what do they know? They are outdated and stuck in their old ways; they are obsolete, uninformed, and ignorant of what is best. Being old, they have become unfruitful and non-progressive, and they are disrupters of the new that desires to sprout!"

This is not another truth but the truth.

The new is excellent when it does not disregard the wisdom, experience, principles, and teaching of the old. The old is excellent when it does not stifle, ignore, disregard, or place roadblocks in front of the new. Both have their place, and we would be wise to understand the value of both perspectives.

Progress and evolution are byproducts of symbiosis between the old and new when tied to fundamental, unchanging, proven truth.

Opinions and science change and thus should not be considered absolute or final truth. Both could be true at any given time but may not be the ultimate, enduring truth of the matter.

Perhaps the difference between something being true is the test of time. Something can be true in a moment because of what we know about it, but *ultimate* truth is unchanging.

There is no other truth.

Truth from days past includes and embodies the old while paving the way for the new. The saying goes, "It was true back then, it is true now, and it will be true in the future."

Something can be true but not truth.

Rejecting and disliking something or someone based on opinion, preference, personal experience, history, or culture is not founded in truth. Each of these attributes varies based on the individual. Given that everyone is different and individual, all can agree on certain things being true but not on what is truth.

Truth cannot be truth if it allows individualism to be viewed as truth. People and their opinions change; they are unstable and not static—characteristics counter to truth.

More truth is not another truth but is very true.

Truth does not change, and ultimately what is true does not change. If something is proven to be true, it will not change.

What is truth? Truth is that which does not change, even if one tries to redefine it.

The laws of gravity stand true in time and space, regardless of what anyone believes, accepts, or knows. If you jump off a building, the truth about gravity will reveal itself. In space, there is another law that is true. Both laws are true at the same time, represent truth in their specific application, and never change nor can be changed.

Truth can be ignored, disregarded, disrespected, and challenged. Truth welcomes testers to prove it as truth.

——————————— **38** ———————————

NOT ANOTHER TRUTH BUT THE PROVEN TRUTH

TRUTH SAYS, "STAND with me or fall standing alone."

Truth says, "No matter how you feel or what you want to believe, you will not stand apart from truth; you will not remain or rise, but eventually you will fail and shall fall."

It has been said that there are two undefeated foes: Father Time and death.

There is a third: truth is inevitable. No matter what you do, how you feel, what you change, or how you are challenged, the truth of what happens and why will eventually be revealed.

Another truth: We struggle with understanding truth by trying to apply it in different ways. We seek to change the meaning of truth to fit our purposes or goals. And if it does not fit, then we resolve that there can be no truth.

To escape the entanglement we have created, consider that truth is not to be defined, redefined, or, if possible, refined but instead discovered! On earth, the reality of gravity cannot be changed or denied. The same applies when exploring space. Most, if not all, things on earth cannot be changed or denied, only discovered. We have, however, modified, merged, misused, and abused things in life, thus creating a change that invariably will lead us to discover some truth.

Discovery of truth happens over time as we uncover the unchanging and enduring truth proven to promote the future and move beyond the past.

What is true at the time of discovery or experience must be proven before one can conclude that it is truth. We must be cautious of our human inadequacies. What has been discovered or uncovered is only true once it has been tested over time.

Consider that the one great test of truth is sustainability. Does what is being offered as truth remain the same over time? Does it apply universally? Can one's thinking, opinion, thought process, and conclusions stand the test of time? It is likely truth if it is sustainable and the outcome does not change.

When considering truth, the only challenge should be whether to accept or reject it. One can ignore the truth, but truth never needs to defend itself; the outcome proves what is true.

This can be tested in the statement, "I was born that way." History validates, and science cannot deny, the basis and basics of life on planet Earth. Living things fall into various categories such as mammals, reptiles, plants, insects, and sea life, and each has subcategories. Some nuances have been discovered, but the categories remain the same, as they represent the truth.

For example, a plant has never been categorized as a reptile, nor has a sea creature become an insect. While it is true that man can interrupt, alter, or manipulate biology, what was changed was not that way originally.

Within certain categories in creation, changes in the creature's sex anatomy have been discovered. It must be noted that when specific plants or creatures change in this way, it is to enable reproduction. These changes are based on certain conditions in their environment, not a choice.

We know this to be truth, as the basis of choice is self-awareness, and only humans are self-aware. As such, humans make decisions.

What is truth? Truth first reveals that no one can reproduce in and of himself or herself. Truth reveals that no two species that are the same gender can reproduce. Truth reveals that the only way to affect this truth is for humans to alter what was natural.

Another truth is that humans have free will, being born that way.

We discover and have abilities. We are given options with cautions and even restrictions. With some discoveries, we come to learn the truth through misuse or abuse; with other discoveries we have been given the consequences of exercising free will in a way that violates the truth.

Another truth: As much as we love, expect, and even demand the freedom to make choices, there are unexpected, unintended consequences. Free will enables independent thinking.

With free will, we start with what we believe to be truth. Then we *should* subsequently consider the outcomes of what we believe to be true. But our free will left unchecked or left to itself is just that, our freed will. Our will is free of having any regard for truth. Everything, or at least what is most important, is no longer under any control. The "will" has been set free, and being freed, there is no "will" to regard truth.

The old and new must realize that they have a common need: wisdom. The old has done things that the new realizes lacked wisdom, and the new is attempting to do things that the old realizes lack wisdom.

There can be no truth absent of wisdom, as wisdom is the proof of truth. Wisdom would say to the foolish, "That is not wise." Foolishness is proven by its folly, and wisdom calls it out.

For truth to be truth, it must be self-validating, meaning it must successfully be time-tested and perpetually remain true. For something to be true, it must also withstand the question, "Is this true regardless of time, circumstance, situation, and even opinion?"

There is an ethical truth that continues to echo. Ethical truth must survive all scrutiny and challengers and stand the test of time. To be truth, it must be sustainable and reproductive. That which is false ultimately cancels itself out over time, as its goal is to remove. Ethical truth would say, "It is true that something may cancel itself and in doing so be truth." In this case, it is a truth that endures but is not sustainable or reproductive.

If that which is not good is successful over time after eliminating everything it faces, then it will have to face itself and answer the very questions it asked of others: Why you? What makes you right? Who are you?

If cancer had its way without challenge, it would wipe out all life and then, being the only cell remaining, would have to face itself and in doing so would become nonexistent, because it is cancer. That is a true statement, but it is not sustainable. If unchecked, cancer destroys the body and then dies in that body and no longer exists.

Another truth: Truth, it could be said, is life-sustaining. That which is true is life-experiencing. With this application, it would be false to say that cancer has anything to do with truth other than that it destroys.

Cancer in the body dies after it has destroyed the body. When there is no life, the cell will either turn on itself or die from having no more life to destroy.

We would not consider something true if it destroys life. We would not only ask who wants to hear that kind of "truth," but we would run from it, ignore it, or dismiss it, since it destroys. If something is truth, we must consider whether it is a truth worth learning and knowing. We want to hear truth that promotes life!

Another truth: The truth cannot die. Some ideas are not truth, as they are not sustainable. Over time, the idea said to be true will destroy. After eliminating everything in its path, it will ultimately eliminate itself, as there is nothing left to destroy. The so-called true idea dies, as it is not truth.

Another truth: The idea of same-sex relationships being equal to male-and-female relationships is incongruent. The same sex of anything cannot reproduce if they mate, and left to itself, it would self-terminate. If everyone's parents were attracted to the same sex, no one would exist, as their parents would not have been able to produce them.

Another truth: We, in our humanity, discriminate and look to purge anything that we do not understand, does not look like us, or is a threat to us. Yet if everyone looked the same, we would still establish a hierarchy; we would look for differences.

Another truth: That which seeks to end or eliminate life cannot perpetually produce and therefore is not life. Being on top requires domination and, if need be, elimination. In either case, you are not producing.

If you are pressed to produce from a place of domination, then you will become oppressive! You can say and believe you are on top, but if you are the oppressor, whatever is driving you is on top. Whatever has control over you is in control, not you.

Another truth: The person or thing truly on top does not have to force or prove anything, as they are on top.

Though often challenged, truth does not need to engage, embrace, or consider everyone's opinion or experience to be truth. Truth is not obligated to defend itself. If a truth is to be unseated, the obligation falls on the shoulders of the challengers to disprove it. Moreover, if they are successful, it was not the truth but either a truth or something true once.

To be truth, it must accurately report or reflect what is actually and verifiably true. An additive to truth is life, things that are sustainable.

Another truth: If a person is doing something erroneously on the job, things ultimately will fail. Things will not work out, the assembly line will stop, and the doors will close because what has happened cannot stand the truth test. The truth shows in the person doing the job correctly, the customer returning, and things generally working well.

We find three truths juxtaposed:

1. If the entire population was in same-sex relationships, there would be no reproduction, and life would cease. It would be "cancel culture."

2. The elimination of plant life in the name of progress as we erect buildings would, over time, irreparably harm the earth and perhaps be the cause of our demise. Eliminating plant life while buildings stand is fueling climate change.

3. If we create artificial intelligence intended to make life better and believe that one day it will be able to think, reason, and learn independently and advance beyond its man-made abilities, then what is created will be greater than its creator. If that were to happen, life would cease. (Many sci-fi movies, such as the appropriately named *Terminator*, have been based on that very impossibility.) This is creator change.

Another truth: We can all be wrong, but we cannot all be right. Everyone cannot be right at the same time. It may be true that we are different; it may be true that we disagree, and it may even be true that what we disagree on is true for us at that time. It is, therefore, *a* truth—it may be *my* truth or *your* truth, but it is not necessarily *the* truth.

One person sees the cup half full, another sees it half empty, and yet another just sees the water because they are thirsty. Each scenario is true, and all are true to each person—that is until questions are asked to determine what is actual truth. There is a difference between what is "true" and what is "truth." Now that's the truth!

Another truth: Truth asks, "If I were the target of a specific truth, would I have an objection, and if so, why?" Truth asks, "Does your position that is considered true promote, advance, support, and/or sustain life?"

Another truth: Renaming something that destroys life to pass laws does not change the truth that it is murder.

Another truth: Scientists have reported that the universe continues to expand. With such expansion, there is a guess that there are different forms of yet-to-be-identified life.

The mere fact that "science" is reporting that the universe is expanding validates the "truth" that truth is connected to life, reproduction, and sustainability.

The universe is not dying or shrinking. Although certain celestials have imploded or exploded and are nonexistent, the universe continues to grow and expand. It might be that the things that have died and now cease to exist served their purpose and could not contribute to the continued expansion. But they were not exterminated.

Another truth: The only acceptable reason to remove something or someone is if it intends or desires to extinguish the process of replication and is anti-life. The elimination or removal of that which destroys, such as diseases, viruses, and animals that kill humans, is a promotion of life. Life and reproduction are not regulated solely by choice; rather, true life is where there is no choice in the equation. Animals mate, and humans choose their mates, both by choice. Neither is drawn to the same sex to create life.

Truth separates differences to get to the truth, as differences are usually based on opinions, preferences, agendas, and choices, with an eye toward the beholder's desired outcome.

Truth is based on facts that cannot be denied. Truth is devoid of feelings, opinions, and even experiences, as your experiences may reveal what is true to you but not the truth. Truth can be found if it is understood and accepted for what it is, not what someone would want to make it.

Truth: If you voluntarily put your head in a bucket of water, eventually, you will instinctively pull your head out because your lungs will compel you to gasp for the available air.

Truth: If it did not work for a good reason in the past, it will not work for a good reason today. Hating and enslaving people who do not look or believe like you is a waste of opportunity and responsibility. They are people, and eventually, they will break free of your chains.

Truth: There is a difference between what I choose to say I am and what I am. Truth says a male is a male and a female is a female based on their anatomy. The animal kingdom has no confusion in this matter. Truth says that if someone is born with more than one sex organ, that person has a physical anomaly or abnormality. We would look at physical contributions to the anatomy other than just the primary sex organ relied on to quickly identify gender.

This condition is rare historically, and it is medically possible to determine which sex organ is extraneous based on other physiological factors. The point in these matters is to get to *the* truth, not *a* truth.

Truth isn't what I decide or have been made to believe. "My" truth is not "the" truth. I can look in the mirror and chant all day every day that I am a monkey because I was raised in the jungle; I may even think and/or feel like a monkey. However, it is clear that I am not a monkey; I am a human being. My self-perception may have been marred, but I do not have the anatomy and other attributes of a monkey.

With all of man's efforts, evolution, and progress, truth cannot be created. It can only be discovered. We can attempt to change someone or something, but that does not change the truth about that person or thing.

Truth always presents itself as a mirror. You can accept or reject what you see.

The mirror of truth says, "I know how you feel, but this is who you are." Accepting ideas that are not rooted in the truth is dangerous because we are the ones who are deceived.

The truth remains unpolluted.

It was once said, "If you believe it, it is not a lie."

What is not being said is, "A lie is a lie, even if you believe it."

Even if the lie does not lie down, the truth will stand!

A statement made a long time ago, the irreducible minimum, "You will know the truth, and the truth will set you free."[1]

If you are entangled, unsure, or at an end that does not result in freedom, you can be certain that you have not discovered truth!

—————— 39 ——————

BY DESIGN—THE HUMAN RACE

WE ARE ALL similar. We have two arms, two legs, two eyes, one nose, two ears, two lungs, and one heart. When something is visibly missing, we say the person has a disability. If someone has something extra, such as six fingers or toes, we call that an abnormality. We may even push the envelope, perhaps errantly, and use the term *deformity*.

A disability or deformity a person is born with or that occurs due to an accident is not a choice. Often those with a disability or deformity would correct the anomaly if they could.

The differences and disabilities that should not be part of conversations about diversity, inclusion, and belonging are the ones that result from a person's choice rather than by God's design, an accident, or human influence. This is especially true when someone born one way feels compelled to change themselves, saying they had no choice but to fix what they felt was broken or wrong.

Overcoming a disability is not the same as overcoming a deformity, especially a self-inflicted deformity. The disabled are to be applauded and given opportunities to be who they have been created to be. Making changes because one desires to do so is not a disability. When something is changed from its original form, it could be labeled as deformed.

Efforts to change the baseline definitions of *disabled* and *deformed* are leading to the undoing of our society. When something is changed by choice, that something becomes deformed, and we disable its original God-design. We have imposed our choice.

People come in all shapes and ethnicities and have vast differences in competencies. The earth has been made for us to enjoy, and the earth itself is diverse. The variations in colors and competencies wipe away the dull, predictable, and mundane and enable imagination, creativity, and progress. One person is skilled at this and another at that—a diversity of skills makes the world go around. A lack of diversity would equal a lack of discovery and progress. When everyone fulfills their God-given purpose to the best of their abilities, the whole of society will benefit.

Have you noticed that, by and large, the sky is rarely devoid of clouds? Of course, there are certain regions of the world where the sky always seems to be blue and cloudless. However, I have noticed, that when you look up, every day the sky is different. No sky is ever the same except when there are no clouds, and the cloudless days make the cloudy ones different.

The sky is a vast, ever-changing canvas that is never replicated. Even a blue sky is only blue in certain areas. This is by design. Much like snowflakes and fingerprints, no two expanses of the sky are ever the same. To further the diversity, the clouds fill the sky, and the sun illuminates those clouds differently by the hour and by the day, giving the appearance of a painting. Then there is a different illumination at night from the sun's reflection on planets and stars that emit their own light. Oh, how diverse the sky, the expanse, and the universe are by design.

Some days I gaze at the sky, with its vast colors and hues, and ask, "How can any day top this one?" Yet another day comes along and indeed does just that, making the previous one a mere memory. It is the variety, the changes in colors in nature, that mark each new season and often bring us joy. Our enjoyment of change is the spice of life that looks so wonderful. The unknown expectation of what's next makes me look forward to waking each day.

The glory of the earth is on great display when it is populated with people who look different and arise with their different capabilities every day. We may perform the same duties and be with the same people, but how we do what we do can never be replicated in exactly the same way, as there are endless variables. We should race to promote and celebrate those differences.

— 40 —

PROGRESSIVE THINKING: WAIT A MINUTE— IT'S NOT THAT SIMPLE

So-called progressive thinking is great, as it is simple in its approach. Although it is great that this thinking is simple, that also is the problem: it is simple in its approach. Progressive thinking does not use the rules of progressive thinking to its end.

Progressive thinking stops short of reason but will argue and insist on its position. Progressive thinking can be summed up in a nutshell, "Agree with our positions or be drowned out by it." It is just that simple. It's a "take no prisoners" approach to cultural change.

While progressive thinking seems great and simple, it is not that simple because progressive thinking is indefensible!

— 41 —

SAME-CHANGE THEORY, PART 1

What would the world be like if everyone was just like you— if everyone was the same? What would the world be like if you could get rid of anything you did not like, anything different or not to your liking, taste, desire, or preference? What would the world be like if there were no choices and everything was always the same?

Why do you season your food? Why do you choose to visit certain restaurants? We have our favorite places that we frequent because we want our food to taste a certain way, the way we remember from our last visit. We hate change on menus, especially changes in our favorite, memorable dishes, because we desire reasonable predictability of our previous enjoyment. We return to experience the same thing.

We don't like when certain menu items have been eliminated, even if they are replaced by something new, as this represents unwanted and unexpected change.

When there is change and we do not get what is expected, the result is disappointment. We think, "What I expected, planned for, and told everyone about has changed, and I hate change. I am disappointed, and so are my guests."

However, as much as we like predictability, what bothers us more than not getting what we expected is boredom from things always being same. We don't like "the same old thing."

We expect what we once enjoyed not to change, but we require new things. As good as our favorite restaurant is, we say, "Let's try a different place; let's go somewhere different!" There is tension between consistency and something becoming stale.

Whether nothing is changing or something is constantly changing, both get old or familiar. When something becomes too familiar, we no longer have zest for that thing because we know what to expect. Although the thing is good, and may even be great, our human nature desires the same but *more*!

The *more* is predictable change. We complain more when things are always the same than when things change! When our technology has not changed, we say it is outdated. As fast as technology advances, we are quick to call something obsolete. As much as we need and enjoy things remaining the same, we also need change.

Change spurs endless possibilities, whereas the same becomes stagnant.

How many people have fallen because they became bored with the familiar, the oh-so-desired predictable? How many men have fallen prey to infidelity because they did not keep things spicy in their marriage? How many women became bored with their husbands, thinking, "That is just how he is; he will never change"? How many wives would prefer that their husbands were consistently inconsistent or predictably unpredictable?

There is a struggle where we dislike and resist change. We secretly pursue change out of necessity, as without change, life becomes boring, and meaning and purpose dim beyond visibility.

Without change, we lose the ability to focus. It is suggested that the eye, if set on one thing without change over a lengthy, uninterrupted period, slowly loses the ability to see clearly. Changes in perception, depth, color, and size all contribute to an eye being healthy and staying sharp and in better focus. As the eye adjusts to what it sees, it experiences beneficial changes in its composition. Thus, we could say change is necessary to be healthy. The eye remains the same, but there are changes that make the eye the eye.

Similarly, if where we lived was the same and everything looked the same, our vision would dim from seeing the same thing all the time. Change is the needed zest and spice of life, as change represents diversity. The same change theory is this: the essence never changes; it always remains the same yet allows for a change in how it expresses itself.

Same changes are the critical attributes of diversity and inclusion. Protecting and keeping what was originally intended, created, and envisioned the same in its essence while allowing enhancements are the critical attributes of diversity and inclusion. A car is a car, and a truck is a truck, but both are modes of transportation. We don't redefine what transportation is but allow and even promote model variations. We don't call a house or a sofa a mode of transportation to be inclusive. And if it were possible for a painting to talk, we would reject the notion that a painting is just a painting.

In creation, there are different kinds of animals, plants, trees, creatures in the sea, and birds in the air. Each creature has variations in species; they have different expressions but are the same.

— 42 —

SAME-CHANGE THEORY, PART 2

CHANGE AS A result of diversity and inclusion is the spice of life! We accept and enjoy differences and recognize through inclusion the benefit of things and people being different. A diversity of colors paints the canvas of our world with such beauty that seeing only black and white ceases to suffice. Nostalgically, the purist enjoys going into the archives and viewing the black-and-white movies, remembering "back then." One hundred percent of the time there is a return to full color in our pursuit of a higher definition based on the most recent technological changes.

Seeing our world and one another in color versus only in black and white is the proper view of diversity and inclusion. When we embrace same change, we begin to see things with 20/20 vision. When we hold true to this definition, we experience superior 20/10 vision. All things are in focus, not blurred but in full, HD color—all the same but inclusive of innate changes.

Having almost infinite possibilities of color is far better than only black and white. A test of preference: Would you prefer a box of crayons with only your favorite color, just black and white, or limitless colors? If you said you would want only your favorite color, how long would it take you to become bored with that one color and seek out at least one other crayon? If you kept your favorite and added just one more, how long would it take you to become bored? The cycle would continue, which is why endless possibilities are the best option.

The box of crayons represents the same-change theory, or diversity and inclusion. The crayons are the same, but the colors are different (representing the same change), and because the crayons are diverse, all should be included.

The concepts of diversity and inclusion are much more substantial than the idea of everyone being the same. Few colors juxtaposed to the many would be like comparing a candle to the sun. Put a candle in front of the sun, and you will no longer see the candle.

If our society departed from the divisiveness of seeing just one or a few skin colors, we would benefit from the diversity surrounding us. The light from one candle still shines, but it is even brighter when it joins the many.

The same-change theory is the embodiment of diversity and inclusion. It emphasizes the context of same change, noting that the change is in expression, not essence. The essence cannot choose.

It should be noted when debating the evolutionists and progressives that if a change occurs that impacts someone's essence, it is by creation, not choice. A worm goes into a cocoon and becomes a butterfly. This is because the worm was created to do that. A fetus in the womb develops into a child. The essence of the human is not changed; it is just being expressed differently.

Same-changing is when the original remains true to itself but changes or grows, reflecting its original self. It is in the context of this diversity that all should be included. Perhaps the two greatest seasons on the calendar are spring and fall, when the infinite colors of nature are displayed in their ever-changing glory. The same old same old is the perfect picture of diversity and inclusion—the same changing. Nature is always changing, but it is still always nature. The changing color of the leaves and sky occur as a result of them being what they were created to be. This includes how the leaves and sky interact with other elements or things. They all hold true to how they were created.

Same-change theory advises the importance of not distorting the picture of diversity and inclusion with choice. Everyone has preferences and the right to see things differently—this is a God-given right. As a result, decisions are made for various reasons and often simply due to one's life experiences.

We all have the DNA, but even that is diverse and different. Our core DNA is still DNA even if there are variations. Even if we make changes, our DNA remains the same.

There are acceptable and needed changes to correct decisions that are detrimental to life, society, and even self. At times, life changes must be made to return to what we know as life's original, intended purpose. While life's intended purpose can be argued, it is both the lack of choice and the impact of choices that do not reflect a person or thing's intended purpose. Life's intended purpose is to promote life.

We all desire, need, and pursue attaining, achieving, and actualizing who we were designed to be. We live with purpose, reflecting that design. No one wants to be in bondage; we all seek freedom. We all innately seek life, even if it is simply self-preservation, possibly at others' expense.

It is true that one can be a product of their environment, but such truth does not negate how the person was born. We are all the same and capable of changing.

Even with all the changes, one common denominator remains, though it is often debated. The common reality we all share, never to be changed though we try, is that everyone has been made, formed, shaped, or created. We all are created, and we all are unique in design, not by decision.

Our choices should not be equated to design; thus, it should not be said that we are born that way. We are free to make decisions and even come to conclusions outside the voice and values of the One who is over all creation.

Our Creator has a set of morals, values, and standards. How I feel and my experience in life may be in opposition to those morals, values, and standards.

Some may have the conviction that "I was born this way; this is the way I feel." It is dangerous to base how you feel, or have been made to feel by your environment or society, on something you can choose.

When it is said, "I was born that way," the purpose is to reflect who you are without any human influence, interference, or impact. The purpose of the seasons of life, from childhood to older adulthood, is to express that we human beings are the same, even though we change. We don't change from humans to something else, nor did we change from monkeys to humans.

Allowing infinite expressions of our essence delivers the colors of the picture in high definition. We can bring our essence into focus for all to see without the distortion of influence by man or choice.

Color never chooses its color; it only displays it. Mankind may mix colors by choice. The result is a new color. It is still color but expressed differently. To be fruitful and multiply is the charge given to man, with no prohibition based on skin color. The world is filled with diverse colors. None are to be put down or made to be less; all colors are equal in and of themselves. They are the same but different.

Together the diverse colors make up a limitless palette, where boredom can find no place, and the picture can be celebrated in its fullness.

The wonderful differences represented among us are necessary and great, as they are the spice of life. Change is at its height, its pinnacle, when it reflects the original. This is especially true when something changes after being influenced by man and returns to its intended purpose. We rightfully celebrate when someone in bondage becomes free and realizes their potential. They are the same person but now are changed, and this change sheds light on what it means to be a human being who is free and productive.

Beneficial change does not seek to alter the original intent. We are free to make decisions, but we are not given authority to redefine original intent and change the intent by saying, "I was born this way."

Diversity and inclusion are intended to lead the way by removing obstacles imposed on people who have no choice in how they were brought into this picture—i.e., by removing the things that weigh people down. People who claim they are "born this way" are released from the pressures brought on by these errant, misguided, self-harming injustices that can be remedied. This is diversity and inclusion: Recognizing that some are born one way and change as a result of being created differently is inclusion. Being made different but not by any influence of man is diversity.

We all are born the same, and being the same, we are to be included. We are to promote, accept, and embrace diversity, reflecting and celebrating being the same but not identical. This is the same-change theory.

43

EVOLUTION, INCLUSION, AND THE DECONSTRUCTION OF DIVERSITY

L ET US LEAN into a discussion regarding diversity.
Evolution and progress have evolved to the point of digression. Many opinions, both offered and accepted, are integrated into the fabric of our society. We can clearly see there is more unrest in the world and in people's lives, not less.

The more we say that what is chosen is equal to what is natural and objectively true, the more disruption and confusion there is.

Unrest is upon us because we have changed what once was clear and self-evident by redefining the terms. We have effectively redefined what was once considered reality and created a new reality. The new reality, however, is not self-evident but rather self-imposed. Our new, redefined reality reflects our wants, desires, and popular opinion. While opinions are the privilege of all, when opinions are accepted without being tested against a self-evident standard, the result is the deconstruction of society.

Changing how one feels, which is afforded by the privilege of choice and offered as an opinion in the name of evolution, has proven itself to be the root of our unrest. It is to be noted that evolution does not occur as the big bang theory claims, when something suddenly emerges out of nothing! As sudden as it seems, our unrest is a slow, calculated, little-by-little strategy. Certain ideas have taken over simply because they have been allowed to be present.

Let the weed grow slowly. Get people used to seeing it. Entertain conversations claiming the weed is part of the garden, and if it is treated differently from the other plants, label that as hatred, ignorance, and a lack of progressive thinking. The weed must be treated "properly," and it reflects poorly on us if we don't accept the weed being in the garden. Although the weed has a history of overtaking the garden and killing everything in its path, progressive thinking welcomes the weed.

The weed, as it seeks to take over and take no prisoners, effectively blurs the lines. It does so to the point where the natural barriers established to effectively govern are framed as non-progressive, if they are not entirely eliminated. In the name of diversity, inclusion, and progressive thinking—a concept that sounds good but is designed to make those who disagree with it seem backward—the weed's agenda is to push until it prevails. The pushing has resulted in the allowance of continued adjustments to natural laws, making lawlessness the new norm. The new norm is progressive thinking and evolution proclaimed and explained.

As society continues to adjust, reconfigure, redefine, and add so many letters to the identity acronyms in the name of progressive thinking that we will soon exceed the English alphabet. We can map a direct path to unrest. Even proponents of adding letters would admit this. They will not admit, however, how progressive thinking and its evolution have contributed to the current state of affairs.

It is not incidental that as we have "evolved," our society has devolved. Some would say this just so happens to be and is not a result of our so-called evolution. Progressive thinking and evolution agree with the possibility of unintended consequences, but not how they contribute to those consequences. Progressive thinking and evolution never consider that their position or agenda could be something other than good. After all, if it were bad, it would not be called progressive.

So they say, "Anyone who disagrees with our position is not progressive."

Progressive thinking does not want to progress, move forward, and improve! Its categorization, forced by the weed, is the heart of the takeover.

It is not the number of people in the fight that matters to progressive thinking or evolution but the number of letters added to the acronyms. The progressive-thinking agenda says, "We don't need many who are the same but rather a lot who are different, creating a new group. We add people with various differences to our numbers to make the group larger." Progressive thinking and evolution promote having a group of people who all are the same by being able to change at will based on how they feel. However, they say they change to match how they were born. "We add more letters, adding to the acronyms to ensure everyone is included. In doing so, no one is offended, as choice has been added to the mix."

The ingredient of choice is good for an individual's or some individuals' tastes. Still, it is a bad recipe for any continued, predictable, sustainable outcome. The recipe continues to change, as do the tastes, and so does the outcome. As society continues to evolve, being progressive as it is, one never knows what they will get!

Inclusion and diversity statements we have come to accept, embrace, and even celebrate are based on differences assigned by choice, not birth. How I feel has been redefined by society, popular *vote*, new laws, and the like. This does not mean a person was "born that way," or born with an identity based on how they feel.

Consider a thief. If a thief said he has always felt like stealing and was born that way, hopefully someone would have the courage to respond, "You may feel that way, but you have a choice in the matter."

I'm hoping we would hear: "You must restrain yourself. You were not born that way, but you can do something about it even if you feel that way." If no one would say these things to a thief, the authorities of a rational society would say, "We don't care how you feel!"

The laws of virtually any society likely would never be rewritten to accept the idea that thievery is acceptable because the lawbreaker claimed to be born that way.

With all of our evolution, what once was clear has become blurred due to open-ended, unrestrained, undefined, unrestricted inclusion. The result is simply figurative and real free falls.

Once clear but now blurred is the idea that there should be no discrimination. In correcting the wrongs of the past, progressive thinking is doing a great disservice. It was necessary to right the wrongs but not to create new rights.

One person thinks someone born a specific way, who had no choice, should be invited to the table. Another believes a person who does not have a particular skill set should also be in the conversations of inclusion but not always at the table. We rightly discriminate, as we would not put a scalpel in the hands of an unskilled person or allow someone who is not qualified to pilot an aircraft. We do this not based on whether someone was born a certain way but on ability. In addition, it can be said that one is not like the other. No one is better, but one is more qualified or fit.

Progressives have now blurred even the definition of discrimination. In its basic essence, discrimination is making a distinction.

Progressive thinking has evolved, forcing the diversity discussion to add letters: DEI (diversity, equity, and inclusion), B (belonging), and A (acceptance). This is designed to no longer make a distinction in the name of diversity but rather to just include all people and treat everyone the same, regardless of their choices.

DEI is intended to ensure there is no distinction among those who have no choice in the traits that make them a minority. Appropriately, making such a distinction would be the basis of rightfully discriminating to correct the wrongs of the past.

Discrimination's dark side is in the *treatment* of distinction. We have treated people born with no choice as being less than and not the same. An easy example is the treatment of women. They are the same and yet different from men, and as a result of their distinction they are discriminated against.

DEI (diversity, equity, and inclusion), DEB (diversity, equity, and belonging), DEA (diversity, equity, and acceptance) ensure God-given equal treatment while remaining mindful of appropriate distinctions.

The one allowable discrimination is the distinction between being "born that way" and choice. In the name of evolved, progressive thinking, choice has been made equal to no choice. With this application, "choice" says, "Treat each person as born that way."

The slope is slippery and dangerously destructive.

What was once clear but is now blurred is that a choice should not create division or discrimination. While progressive thinking says there should be no discrimination, clear thinking says there should be.

Our era of progressive thinking has resulted in a world where reality is tied to and based on feelings.

There are limits, but those too are based on how society or an individual feels at any moment. Yet again, this is why the slope is not just slippery but dangerous and destructive.

The experiences of life in our society prove this to be true, even though truth itself is being redefined, ignored, eliminated, or viewed as being plural. They say, "There are many truths: your truth is your truth, my truth is my truth, their truth is their truth, and all can coexist."

THE RESULTS OF EVOLUTION, OR PROGRESSIVE THINKING

The jury has returned. We now know that while on the surface redefining choice sounds and looks good, society can only be sustained by discrimination based on choice.

A society that does not discriminate between choices and seek a distinction between choice and no choice is doomed. We know what to expect of a society that has no discrimination of choice and respect of birth history: we destroy others and ourselves!

Regardless of feelings, what one may have the propensity to do, or how one is convinced they were born, our actions are still the result of personal choice. We have a choice—which presents itself simultaneously in virtually every situation—to do good or no good.

In our new, progressive world, we have evolved to where we even get to choose the definition of good and bad.

THE LINES FURTHER BLURRED ...

Our conscience, which differs among us all, is shaped by our experiences. Our conscience regulates our interpretation of what is good and bad and what is and is not done by choice. You choose to listen to or ignore what was formulated in your conscience by choice, fueled by preference or feelings. When we reach into our conscience, tapping into it for clarification or decision-making, we do so to make a choice based on how we feel, not how we were born.

The conflict of conscience results from feelings or choices set against reality: I may feel this way, but this is the way things are, and therefore, I am conflicted. To resolve the conflict, the claim is that feelings are not choices; they are the way things are. Yet "the way things are" has changed our society, and "the way things are" is causing division, distrust, dislike, and unrest. Admitting or grafting choice into the matter has resulted in how things are.

THE FIX …

The ultimate fix for the dilemma of choice and the conflict of conscience is a renewed mind. This is a mind and conscience that chooses to rely on that which is greater than it is, that which does not change, that which remains stable even when things change. The only choice to be made is to rely on the plumb line or to measure your choices against the plumb line.

Choice must not be part of the conversation of inclusion and diversity unless measured against the plumb line of diversity, inclusion, and belonging. These are to be protected based on "being" by birth, not by choice.

Society might say that someone who was influenced by their culture to become a pedophile, rapist, or thief was forced to be the way they are. From what happened to them, they made choices, or choices were made against them, but they were not born that way. No way!

THE ARGUMENT …

Indulge a train of thought for a moment. Let us say the pedophile, rapist, or thief was born that way. If a person was born that way and had no choice, are we not penalizing them for something they have no control over?

If so, shouldn't we release the pedophile, the rapist, the thief—virtually anyone behind bars who professes to have been born in some way that caused them to engage in criminal activity? Did they have a choice in the matter? Should we not integrate them into society in the name of diversity and inclusion?

It is being suggested in the name of DEI, DEB, and DEA that they should be included and have the same rights, since they were born that way. In the name of choice, can we also claim to know how someone identifies? A person might say, "I get to tell you how I was born! I have the prerogative to decide what I was at birth, as this can change based on how I feel."

If at some point a person feels one way, and then later things change and they feel another way, the sad reality of our society and our so-called progressive thinking is that what "way" someone was born is subject to change.

Houston, we have a problem!

ENLIGHTENMENT ...

Just because someone says, "I was born this way, feel this way, have discovered my 'real' self, and therefore resolve I was made this way, with no choice in the matter," that does not negate what is seen in the mirror. Those who say, "Look in the mirror at what you see, at what is," would be characterized as ignorant, bigoted, divisive, hateful, or non-progressive.

The mirror that accurately reflects how one was born is devoid of opinion. It reflects actions that are a byproduct of being born a certain way. The mirror reflects the physical reality, leaving them no choice or ability to be swayed by societal influence.

Doing something by choice is not always the same as doing something by desire. It can mean doing something by force. "I choose to do this or that, though I don't specifically desire to do so; this has been forced on me, as it is my only option or choice." If there is only one good option, it cannot be said, "That was my choice," but it can be said, "That was my only choice!"

When something is forced on a person and is not their choice, they can be made to become something they would not have chosen. They still were not "born" that way but "made" that way, not by choice or desire. And, frankly, if there had been another choice or a better choice, that is what they would have chosen!

When there seems to be no other option or way out, we are forced to choose or accept the condition. These acts of choice often are fueled, influenced, driven, and/or shaped by horrible experiences akin to the blind/hurt leading the blind/hurt. Many choices are fostered, influenced, politicized, and even blamed on religion, resulting in hate of oneself as originally made, others (because the person believes others hate them), and anyone else who does not accept the condition.

Diversity and inclusion are not to be a denial of truth and reality. That would lead to anarchy and the destruction of individual ideals, truth, meaningfulness, purpose, sustainability, and ultimately life.

Within the context of inclusion and diversity, saying, "I was born this way" based on feelings and choices that result from experiences means we should accept riots and hatred. Why not? Aren't those who riot and hate born that way? Why are you keeping them out, arresting them, charging them with wrongdoing when they are being themselves, how they were born? Our laws and society would even say, "I don't care how you [the critic] feel."

Actions are a result of feelings. If we accept choices made based on sexual feelings or an orientation, then we must accept the feelings or orientation to destroy, riot, and tear things down things because of feelings!

This cannot be!

If the rioter was born this way, then in the name of inclusion and diversity, they should *not* be kept out, but should be welcomed to the party. There are no crimes against society if a person can claim they were born in a way that causes them to riot. If they have no choice, they have committed no crimes, as they had no choice but to be who they are and, therefore, should be included. We must demonstrate equity.

With this thinking, Hitler should be invited to the party. He would tell you he did not choose to commit genocide; he was "born that way." If we do not accept that he was born that way, perhaps we would say he was made that way, but still, he had no choice, right? Our progressive thinking has brought us to the point that all are entitled to the same benefits. Progressive thinking wants society to treat those who make choices as the same as those who are mistreated. Who are we to cast Hitler out in the name of being progressive? Don't we want to foster inclusion and diversity?

If a person says, "I feel like killing people, raping women, hanging out with children, and engaging in sex acts with animals," why should they not be included in DEI? After all, that person would tell you, "I have no choice in the matter. I was born this way!"

DEI, DEB, and the entire family of inclusive acronyms are not viable or sustainable based on choice. It becomes, and will remain, an endless, slippery, destructive slope when choice is allowed into the conversation. We change as our choices change and as a result of influences, experiences, and feelings, which is the very reason personal choice devalues, dilutes, and disarms this new idea of inclusion.

Choice, therefore, should never be part of the conversation when discussing DEI and DEB, as diversity and inclusion are intended to discriminate between what should not be treated as choice and what should be.

DEI and DEB are at their best when they are representative and present as equal all who have no choice.

"Made that way" is not "born that way." "Treated that way" is not "born that way." Because feelings change, feelings do not reflect reality; therefore, "feeling that way" does not mean "born that way."

DEI and DEB have no end and can never fulfill their goal without boundaries.

You were made as you are, I was made as I am, and we are equal—different but equal. Difference is at the heart of DEI and DEB; being equal but different does not happen by choice. The differences, though the parties are equal, are to be included. The diversity of "different but equal" is DEI/DEB.

It is a crime to diversity, equity, inclusion, and belonging when we see people in locked arms proclaiming the same message, asking to be treated the same, and asking for the same rights or entitlements as those whose actions are not based on a choice.

A person who chooses a particular lifestyle, as long as it does not break the law, is free to do so. However, that person should not be given the same treatment as those who have no choice in the matter. Give them a treatment based on choice, not their birth.

While choice is to be rejected in the conversation of inclusion, differences are the essence of inclusion and should be embraced, fostered, and celebrated.

Discriminate and *celebrate* that which is by birth. Discriminate and *critique* that which is by choice.

Inclusion and diversity, discriminating between the different that is equal, is what we have been given to bring us together. Our society and progressive thinking have led us down paths that have caused discrimination, which is a distinction intended to recognize that we really are different.

For too many decades, progressive thinking has said that if you are different, it is because you were made different at birth; therefore, people are not all the same. Our society has not only fallen into this trap but now champions such untruths.

Conversations about diversity, equity, inclusion, belonging, and acceptance have been introduced as a necessary, precise, decisive antidote to the woes and unrest experienced in our society in the past and present. The woes and unrest directly result from a lack of inclusion and diversity.

When natural attributes received at birth—absent alterations, societal influences, man's knowledge, or life-changing experiences—are equated with choice, forcing the unnatural upon the natural, it too will lead to unrest and contribute to the woes of our society.

The mountain of inclusion and diversity is steep, and it becomes impossible to climb when you add choice!

44

THE NAKED TRUTH

THE CLAIM ON truth is that you cannot accept the truth! However, when there is no right, everything goes wrong. In addition, if there is no right, then there is no wrong.

The emperor has new clothes. Or, is he wearing no clothes? This world's new reality is confusing; as it may be that the emperor's new clothes are no clothes. The truth is…the emperor is naked!

You may recall the story: "Two swindlers arrive at the capital city of an emperor who spends lavishly on clothing at the expense of state matters. Posing as weavers, they offer to supply him with magnificent clothes that are invisible to those who are stupid or incompetent. The emperor hires them, and they set up looms and go to work." Ultimately, they claim to have finished the emperor's suit and mime dressing him. The emperor walks through the streets naked, and no one will call out the emperor's nakedness except a child. "The moral of this story is that we can't let pride keep us from speaking up when we know the truth."[1]

Over time, in the name of being progressive and politically correct, we have labored to right the wrongs and erase the past by tearing down certain reminders of offenses, memories, misguided actions, and outright ugliness.

One should be ashamed of certain actions of the past, but sadly there remain people who are not. In being remorseful of past actions, the best course is to take actions that demonstrate what should have been or what should be. The only way to change the impact of the past is by doing something different that impacts the present and future and opposes the past, as one cannot change the past.

The downside of forgetting or removing reminders of the past is that it negates one of the best uses of the past, which is to propel us to change and not repeat past mistakes, thus never forgetting to do what is good.

Despite our goodwill, as we march down the road to correct past transgressions, mistakes, or mishaps, we do so misguidedly and recklessly. Many things of the past are worth being reminded of and keeping. But in the process of making progress, we are tearing apart, eliminating, renaming, and redefining many things that proved themselves to be effective, beneficial, and life-giving.

Tearing down images of those who were anti-life is very different from what is happening in society today. The new clothing today is that we are tearing down images of those who oppose those who are anti-life.

We must be more discriminating! Making judgments based on one's feelings and experiences, likes and dislikes is necessary discrimination. Making judgments based on how one has been created and the things one has no control over is the dark side of discrimination.

An opinion is just that—an opinion. While we should perhaps be open to all opinions, opinions are not facts. Many opinions are not thoughtful, and the fact that everyone has one does not mean every opinion has merit. Opinions are personal to the individual and therefore are only true to the individual.

Social media has become the great enabler of opinions. Everyone has a platform to speak their mind or publicly push whatever they want to promote. Free or freed speech is now information pushed out into the public by anyone to anyone.

With our continued march in the name of progressive thinking and evolution, we have seen censorship when a person says something another person believes is destructive or unacceptable. A line has been drawn and is not to be crossed. There is a point we will not cross or allow others to broach. There is a standard, an established or a quasi-plumb line. New clothes are no clothes!

Our new, progressive world has established a standard and agreed with a new plumb line, even if it was done unintentionally. The new standard and plumb line is that there is no standard or plumb line.

The thinking is, "There is no reason if that reason does not fit with my thinking." Society's progressive evolution–based thought process is, "We define what is and is not acceptable. And we get to do so perpetually."

Establishing, defending, promoting, advancing, and living by the premise of deductive reasoning can be pathways to make sense of truth.

Opinions almost always are devoid of any reasoning, and they certainly avoid deductive reasoning. Opinions have no consideration for truth and result in saying instead of hearing, commenting instead of understanding. They say, "I know what I see; I heard what you said, but this is my opinion!"

The question, "What is truth?" is often never answered. It is intentionally ignored, even though it is proven true by what we see (the eye test), what we experience (the social impact test), and what lasts (the test of time).

The most interesting observation in this era of non-truth is that as we profess to be evolving, things are devolving. Regardless of one's opinion, experience, or background, the resounding comment is that our world is not better. There is a problem, Houston!

The argument or debate over what is truth has been carefully misdirected by inserting acceptance as the qualifier, test, or proof of truth. "If it changes, it evolves"—this view captures the current thinking that challenges the past, breaks the old, and cancels culture.

Evolution means that even truth evolves, as we are ever-learning. There is a passage taken from a book of old, the Book of Truth, which deserves attention:

> They are the kind who worm their way into homes and gain
> control over gullible women, who are loaded down with sins
> and are swayed by all kinds of evil desires, always learning but
> never able to come to a knowledge of the truth.[2]

It is said, "I know how you feel, I know what you have been taught, I know what you have been told, and I know what you look like. But that is not true; it was wrong."

The voice of progressive thinking and evolution cries out to get you on its side, championing new truth that, when tested, is no truth. New truth says, "As long as you believe and challenge the old, outdated past, you have successfully evolved."

We must remember that this fast-paced world embraces and accepts constant change as best and normal. Yesterday is obsolete. Accepting any and all differences must be, and therefore shall be, declared the truth.

Evolution and technology have landed us where our evolved thinking, which produced artificial intelligence (AI), has surpassed the truth. We are in an age that ties truth to preferences. We have algorithms to track our patters and conclude that those results are truth.

While AI and this evolution in thinking attempts to be true, it is faulty based on its own standards. The truth of the matter is that we constantly change!

Out with the old, in with new! Out with the old, in with the bold! "Out with the old" does not represent the circle of life. It does, however, reflect the circle in life. Moving on should be done only when it advances. It is not good to move on simply because one does not like where one is.

We quickly forget, disregard, and move on to anything new. We are quick to move on just to say we are moving on or evolving.

People claim to know your preferences, but these are now being confused and all mixed up in the bowl of relative truth. Now your truth is your truth, and my truth is my truth, even if it is proven wrong or plain ridiculous. If it happens to fit the general thinking of society, it must be truth. Why? We say, "Because that's my opinion!"

Truth is now a moving target and has been convoluted. In the name of evolution, truth is now smeared and blurred. It is being challenged and changed based on opinion. Certain ideas are being accepted as truth based on experiences, feelings, and desires.

The naked truth is that there is truth that results in sadness, emptiness, and nothingness. That truth, having accomplished its goal over time, will come to an end, being left to itself, as it cannot produce or reproduce. Although it is truth, it is not the truth that people seek. The only reason one should seek negative, unpleasant truth is to eliminate it.

The naked truth regarding divorce: divorce is the breakup of the union between a man and a woman (male and female, the foundation of the nuclear family), and it is the most egregious form of child abuse.

The naked truth regarding abortion: abortion has an emotional, spiritual, and physical impact that follows the choice of aborting—killing a life that had no choice in the matter.

The naked truth regarding a promiscuous lifestyle: you harm yourself and your partner when there is a physical connection devoid of the emotional (no commitment stated) and spiritual (no commitment cemented).

The naked truth regarding hating your flesh-and-blood brother: hating your brother is a cancer that destroys the carrier and everything it touches.

The naked truth regarding greed: when life is about possessions, the possessor becomes the possessed.

The naked truth regarding truth: work as hard as you like to suppress, ignore, or redefine truth. It will have the last word and prove itself true, outlasting you and your truth.

The naked truth is that you are naked and exposed when you are not clothed with truth that does not change but sustains and adequately covers. The naked truth will protect you from falling for the uncovered lie.

TRUTH

Don't Be Fooled by Foolishness

OPEN COMMUNICATION, CONTINUOUS misinformation, and rapid change have created an unending list of complex social challenges that seem almost otherworldly. Some things seem so out of this world that it's nearly impossible to filter out what is true or not, leaving us vulnerable to utter foolishness.

In the past, there were commonly accepted definitions of right and wrong, acceptable and unacceptable behavior. Today, right and wrong are defined by the individual, and if you don't agree, you are labeled narrow-minded, out of touch, or even worse, evil.

In this section, we look deeper at some of these complex challenges in order to avoid the foolishness of the day.

———— **45** ————

NOTHING IS IMPOSSIBLE

Is it possible to have everything one could ever want or imagine and still have nothing? *Nothing is impossible.*

Is it possible to be imprisoned, not behind steel bars but in concrete high-rises? *Nothing is impossible.*

Is it possible to have so much in your bank account—money to pass on to the fourth, fifth, sixth generation and beyond—that you believe you need no one? *Nothing is impossible.*

Is it possible for your possessions to possess you? *Nothing is impossible.*

Is it possible that having things can blind a person from seeing? *Nothing is impossible.*

Is it possible to have all the things that make one secure but still be in fear? *Nothing is impossible.*

Is it possible to be so sure of ourselves, so sure of our ability, that we do not see our shortcomings? *Nothing is impossible.*

It was once said that it is easier for a camel to go through an eye of a needle than for a rich person to enter the kingdom of God. It was followed by, "What is impossible with men is possible with God."[1] *Nothing is impossible!*

Perhaps there should be impossible things. Maybe it would be to our benefit.

I wish it was impossible to be trapped, deceived, entangled, and undone by my own actions, desires, aspirations, goals, efforts, convictions, beliefs, and wants.

I am saddened that *nothing is impossible.*

—————————————— 46 ——————————————

I'M NEVER WRONG, RIGHT?

IT IS PERFECTLY OK to tell me when I am *right*, and please do so at any time, even if it means interrupting me.

It is never, ever OK to tell me I am *wrong*, no matter the occasion, circumstance, or situation.

It's no good being dead wrong or dead right!

While being right about something may be encouraging and bolster self-esteem, thinking we are always right without the input of others can lead to negative consequences.

How many times have you heard yourself saying, or heard others say, "They are surrounded by a bunch of yes-people who agree to everything they say"?

While no one likes to be wrong, never being challenged or corrected can be unhealthy, and in some cases dangerous.

—————————————— 47 ——————————————

IT IS TRUE, SAYS THE LIE

THE LIE IS perhaps the most potent force on earth.

The lie misleads and misinforms, so much so that a person thinks they want to be caught in its net. The lie is so powerful that it entangles and effectively deceives, resulting in captivity, oppression, and bondage. Consider that few wake up and say, "Let me do something stupid, something that will harm me today or leave me in bondage."

It is almost incomprehensible that someone in bondage would desire to be where they are and have no motivation to be anywhere else. If it is agreed that no one in their right mind desires to be in a cage, before judging those who are addicted or caught up in certain lifestyles, we should first ask ourselves what may have led to their condition.

Why do so many people find themselves in situations and places they do not want to be? Why are so many people not attaining what they desire? Enter the lie!

The lie is so powerful and deceptive that it dismisses those who challenge it and causes those on the receiving end to believe it! The lie is so powerful it can make the majority seem like a minority. More people die for the lie than for the truth. The lie takes no prisoners. It has only cheerleaders!

Those who experience the lie eventually find themselves wishing they had a better option. Once they face reality, regret follows.

When the lie is bought into, the one who has believed the lie thinks there are no other good options and that the lie is the best course to take. The lie also blurs the truth, so no options seem reasonable, logical, or appealing. The lie takes what is good for you and convinces you that it is bad. The lie sells itself by convincing a person that the lie is what they want, and if they attain anything else, they will be lacking. The lie never parades itself as truth; it just tells you everything else is a lie.

Those who would challenge the lie often ask, with bewilderment, "Why do people end up where they are?" They say, "If they don't have the will, if they never come around, then no one can help them."

Observers who challenge those who have bought into the lie often conclude that those duped by the lie are where they are as a result of their own actions. Second, they would say those who bought into the lie did so because of their own weakness. Last, they would argue that it is easier for someone who has been unable to achieve their goals and desires to buy into the lie because they are unsatisfied and thus more susceptible. This is how the lie becomes a plausible alternative.

Critics and naysayers have been so deceived by the lie that they are convinced people are where they are intentionally. Because of this belief, they would say, "You got yourself in—get yourself out." Or, "You made your bed; now lie in it." Such a position implies that people want to be in bondage!

Those bamboozled by the lie are thoroughly convinced that the truth is what the lie claims it to be. Therefore, they believe the lie rather than the truth.

The lie also has trapped the captured into believing they have no way out. They are told they have no control over their lives and no choices in the matters that have them in bondage. The lie even convinces the entangled that they are not trapped. The lie convinces you that you are not in bondage. The lie sears reality so effectively that what once was uncomfortable is now comfortable.

The lie is so insidious that it takes what you want and presents it enticingly but without revealing the entirety of what it will cost you.

The lie is so deceptive that it begs perplexing questions that discerning minds would usually challenge or reject but no longer do. The lie can so perfectly hide its agenda that obvious questions are never asked or pondered. The lie will cause a person to block out the truth, knowing the lie is actually false.

The lie has effectively convinced the larger society that we have no choice in such matters. With such belief the lie conceals how society has come to the place it is. The lie confuses the matter, telling us we have no choice. However, later we look at our world and wonder why things have gotten worse, not better.

The lie sells us on the belief that all is well, but it does not let us know why we are in bondage. The great deception is that we are free, not deceived. We may wonder, "If we are free, why are so many people entangled?" It is because we are trapped by the lie.

The lie deceives, making people think they have no choice in the matter. This prevents them from realizing that they have a choice in all matters.

The lie says when there is no choice, anything goes; nothing matters; everything is relative. "C'est la vie," the lie says, "that's just life."

The lie keeps us from asking why. Given that we have a choice, many of us find ourselves, apparently by choice, in bondage to bad habits and self-destructive behaviors.

The lie says there is no harm done to others, at least no harm we will eventually have to pay for. The lie convinces us that our choice will deliver what we want. Instead, it delivers the consequence of the choice made.

So many people find themselves trapped in a self-destructive cycle. What creates a habit? Masked pleasure blinds the truth and dulls pain in an attempt to eliminate what is causing the pain. The pleasure that feeds the senses draws people into a cycle that never gets them where they truly want to be. There is a quote that says the pleasures of sin will pass.[1] The pleasure passes but rarely does the pain.

Emotional or spiritual pain results from not gaining what one wants and sometimes needs. At times, physical pain manifests when something is lacking emotionally or spiritually.

The lie offers pleasure—getting what one wants or numbing the pain of not getting it—as an alternative. Even when there is a real need, the lie shows up with an alternative to the truth. The lie presents itself as not what was wanted and, frankly, not what was needed.

THE TRUTH ABOUT THE LIE

The lie cannot tell the truth. There is one exception: The lie tells the truth when it reveals itself as a lie. Only then is the lie truthful. However, the lie rarely does this, as its goal is to deceive.

The lie is designed to alter your entire life, to get you off the best course and onto a less desirable course. If the lie cannot destroy, it seeks to get you frustrated so you never become what you have been created to be. The lie will deceive you into enjoying less than you were intended to and sells the alternative as better than the intended.

The lie desires to alter your entire life, with the goal of destroying you. It tells you that God has lied to you and is keeping something from you. The lie claims there is no absolute truth and no one has the right to tell you what to do. The lie promotes hate. The lie creates and fosters conditions that keep a person from being satisfied. The lie plants seeds of dissatisfaction so we think something is always missing, nothing makes sense, and everything is wrong. It is all part of the lie.

The lie makes the abnormal normal. What was once uncomfortable and unacceptable becomes comfortable and acceptable. What once was unsatisfying is now allowed.

Always subtle in its approach but attractive in appearance, the lie is sly, a lightweight in approach but a heavyweight in impact. The lie is overwhelming and all-encompassing when one is sucked in by it.

The lie is substantial but subtle; it is not overt but covert. The lie needs only a little to do a lot. The lie is not small or white; it is an untruth. The lie does not need a breach, just a crack. The lie is so powerful that it requires only the smallest opening to plant doubt.

The lie desires only a slight change of course to impact an entire life. The lie is much like a sea vessel that changes course by one degree and, as a result, is set off course by miles. That one small change will keep a person from ever arriving at their intended destination—and the lie will have won.

The lie says, "Never change your ways, thoughts, beliefs, or course of action." Yet it suppresses the truth that listening to the lie will keep you from achieving your life goals. The lie looks to keep you believing that the road to your destiny will require adjustments but not a change in course.

The lie looks to keep you stuck in your ways. The lie convinces you to be so confident that you never change course.

The lie's greatest deception is to make you think it is not a lie if you believe it. If the lie could ever speak the truth, the aforementioned would be its only truth!

48

YOU BET YOUR BEST LIFE

WHICH ARE RISKIER, taking risks in life with no faith in God or taking *risks* with faith in God?

49

THE ANTI-DILEMMA

WHENEVER IT IS said, "I have a dilemma," the significance of the dilemma is almost always overlooked. The dilemma seems to be minimized. We hear those words and simply walk past, or others hear those words and walk past us.

We should never minimize a dilemma, either when we are facing one or someone else is. Why? A dilemma by definition is "a situation in which a difficult choice has to be made between two or more alternatives, especially equally undesirable ones."[1]

In short, a dilemma is not something a person would want to face themselves or hear that someone else is facing. It is not a desirable place. While a dilemma presents options to choose from, none are desired and don't appear beneficial.

A dilemma presents options that do not feel good or seem to be best and could be unfavorable to the person faced with them. A dilemma in and of itself is not preferred. Yet there is a worse scenario, and that is an anti-dilemma.

What could be worse than being faced with two or more choices, none of which is favorable? Consider being faced with two or more unfavorable choices and therefore creating another option that seeks to avoid the consequences of what is natural. By doing this, a person creates an alternate reality. This state of mind reflects the anti-dilemma. There is a dilemma of choices I don't like, so I create something to escape my dilemma.

There are natural laws, man-made laws, and moral laws. When faced with laws that one might disagree with, the possibility of being faced with a dilemma occurs. The potential way to escape without breaking a law is to create another option from which to choose.

The anti-dilemma is a state of mind, condition, or situation in our world where natural, normal options and the consequences of those decisions are not liked, desired, or accepted. The anti-dilemma is the place we find ourselves in, as we have created a world filled with alternatives that are an abomination to the natural and thus to our society.

50
A CAUSE OF DEPRESSION

HAVE YOU EVER heard someone say, "My truth is my truth; your truth is your truth." You might even agree with that statement.

"There is no ultimate truth," we say, believing this is the only truth regarding truth: that there is no ultimate, stable, end-all-be-all truth.

We think there is no ultimate truth, nor can there be. With this premise, truth changes at one's will. Another truth, even though it is believed that there is no truth, is that we must accept that one can change truth at one's will. Therefore, there is no truth other than truth that can be changed. With no truth other than that, if there is truth, it can be changed. This will make one depressed.

Depression descends in the form of denying an ultimate truth and redefining truth while stating there is no truth. This is cause to be depressed.

In this dialogue, the only truth we agree with is that there is no ultimate truth! We agree, but within this agreement, there is disagreement because while we declare there is no ultimate truth, we have landed on one.

Our ultimate truth is that there is no truth, which is the cause of our depression.

With no ultimate truth and my truth being my truth and your truth being your truth—and both of us having the ability to define and redefine truth—what can free me from the cause of my depression?

SELF-SABOTAGE

We Create Our Own Demons

Living responsibly is much easier than forced accountability, and yet now we live in a world where anything goes and right and wrong are defined by personal preference.

Unless we have a source of truth, we and the people who depend on us the most are at risk. Disregarding accountability creates demons that, once released, are difficult, if not impossible, to control.

In this section, we will look at some of the demons we have created and how to avoid the danger of self-sabotage.

— 51 —

NO LIMITS

IMAGINE A WORLD without limits," a marketing campaign once declared. When those words were heard, there was great intrigue.

Never forget the year 2020. We saw with a clear, twenty-twenty vision what can happen in a world without limits. There was no need to imagine. In that year, the COVID pandemic spread unhindered, possibly because there had been no limits to experimenting and no limits to altering the natural laws of mankind. Having no boundaries and the freedom to cross any line invites disaster.

We have created a world where there is nothing left to imagine. Any content is acceptable. There is no restraint, no such thing as modesty, and censorship has been taken so far out of context that it has no context.

Imagine a world without limits! If nothing else, the COVID pandemic of 2020 is a reminder that a world without limits is dangerous and unsustainable. Social distancing, masks, closed workplaces, etc., were perhaps a needed response to our inability to restrain ourselves.

— 52 —

UNDERFOOT

IT TAKES GREAT effort to keep a person under your foot, trying ultimately to squash them out of existence as they fight back, struggling for their very survival. Yes, it takes great effort and enormous amounts of money, energy, and resources to keep people in bondage instead of simply keeping your foot off them entirely.

Though unproductive, it is amazing how leaders and producers choose to use, and ultimately waste, their energy and resources keeping people underfoot.

If we truly care for others, we will release and resource them to become all they can become rather than keep them underfoot and in bondage to our will.

— 53 —

SEPARATION WITHIN THE CHURCH AND ITS STATE

IT IS ONLY when the separation within the church ceases that the state of affairs will change.

This is the state of affairs. We are living in a time when there is proof that:

- You can have a lot of money, possessions, and power and be poor.

- You can own little to nothing, feel no threat because you have nothing to lose, and still be poor.

- You can seem to be on top of the world and look like you have no worries and still be poor.

What is the state of affairs when it comes to being poor? Poor is the state a person is in when they are unwilling to help prevent someone else from becoming poor.

We would call the person who has little, or who has no possessions at all, poor. Yet the "poor" are almost always willing to share with others in their condition. They are poor in possessions but generous in spirit. From the outside looking in, the poor have nothing, yet they are willing to share.

The person who has much but does not share with those in need is not looking to help others achieve what they have attained. Unable to relate to being in need, they think, "I know where they are, but I cannot identify with them."

Unfortunately, the beat goes on.

There is silence from the majority—not the numerical majority but those with "major" responsibility, the ones with power, possessions, and positions of leadership. There is silence from the majority, those who have. The outrage is coming from those who do not have, the minority.

To experience relief from life's pressures, remember:

- We learn more from what is not said or done.

- We teach by being living examples.

Too often, the majority accepts things even when they are harmful to others. What becomes the norm is then taught; thus they reproduce after themselves.

This is why when CEOs notice their staffs look like them, they say, "I cannot find qualified people other than [the group I'm familiar with]. I've tried, but there are few options." And so the beat goes on.

The *haves* find it easy to follow the beat that beats down progress.

Someone once said you become what you behold. One could add that you become what you behold, especially when you have strategically put in place people who resemble you. We become what we behold, and what we behold we want to maintain. The only change allowed is for the rich to get richer. No change for the poor; they are to remain the same.

The rich remain and get richer, and the poor remain and become poorer, as the beat goes on. Guess who is keeping tempo?

SOCIAL JUSTICE

The Absence of Justice Creates Constant Unrest

THERE IS NOW a constant cry for justice by the very people who create conflict and unrest in the first place. In many cases, justice is now considered injustice as lawbreakers, criminals, and even terrorists cry foul in order to justify their actions.

In this section, we will discuss why the ancient ideal of "do unto others as you would have them do unto you" is still as important as ever, and why some in our society would like to render it obsolete.

—————— 54 ——————

ONE WONDERFUL LUMP OF CLAY

W E ALL HAVE been made from the same lump of clay, but we should never put everyone—based on the actions of one, few, or many—into one lump of clay. We all are human, even if we are not exactly the same. No group is ever entirely the same.

We must fight against believing a majority of the same group is predisposed to certain behaviors and cannot resist themselves. If this were true, there would be no place for the privileged—the *haves*—on the planet.

Neither all the *haves* nor all the *have-nots* are predisposed to any particular behavior. Thus, the notion of lumping all the members of one group into the same category is ill-advised and uninformed.

Extermination, elimination, enslavement, oppression, or incarceration is a zero-sum game. Elimination, oppression, and suppression are the means of annihilation. A few among us are interested in total annihilation, even to their self-destruction. Still, everyone should not be lumped into that one group. One, few, or even many of any group of people do not represent the entire community. You may think you've identified a good sample size, but be careful, as you may find yourself labeled, prejudged, and part of a sample size.

History has informed us that enslavement is not sustainable. There will be either a breakout, breakthrough, or collapse. When everyone around you is gone, the only one left is you. We may hang out in groups, but even within our groups, we tend to have sub-groups, and one day we all will have to deal with ourselves.

The end of all things is when you are the last "one."

55

YOU CAN DEAL WITH THIS, OR YOU CAN DEAL WITH THAT

*S*OCIAL *JUSTICE*: IF those in power do not bring justice to those without power, those without it will look to bring justice to those who have it!

56

MISSING TRUTH

*N*OT TRUE, BUT so true:

Truth: I will accept and embrace the truth I agree with.

Theology: I will accept and embrace the theology that agrees with me.

At a time when people question the existence of objective truth, truth still shows itself to be both true and objective.

Although truth is not always obvious, even when facts are presented, it is verifiable. What is true will always be true, regardless of what we believe or think we believe.

Objective truth also allows for differing opinions and the facts that support them. However, in the end, what is actually true remains accurate, factual, and verifiable regardless of how we view a topic or subject.

57

LABELS

*W*E LOVE ASSIGNING labels to others, but we hate them when we are made to wear them. We say, "I will place labels on others and myself, but no one will place one on me!"

Labels serve one purpose: your own!

What would life be like if we were forced to accept the judgment and labels that others placed on us?

Life would be completely unbearable because we can't possibly live a healthy and productive life based on someone's opinion of who or what we are. However, isn't that exactly what happens when we put labels on others?

Labeling others is a dangerous, misguided proposition because it doesn't take into account their history, experience, or knowledge. More importantly, it disregards their desires about how they want to be perceived. In a word, labels do more damage than good because they not only diminish the person but also distort who and what they might be.

— 58 —

TRIPLE-D DAY: DEFECTIVE DETECTIVE DETECTION

IT'S ONE THING to dislike a particular fruit because of its taste. It's another thing to hate all fruit because you don't like a certain fruit. It is yet another to hate food altogether because you had a bad experience with a certain food or even certain types of food.

If one was injured by an automobile, it would be understandable to be cautious or fearful when driving. It's another thing to say all cars are bad or even to say the brand, make, and model that caused the injury is bad unless the accident was due to faulty manufacturing.

While it is true that an entire series of cars can be defective, leading to a recall, this possibility cannot legitimately be applied to human beings. Such an application should not be made. Humans do not come from an assembly line, and none of them is identical. Even identical twins have differences.

Human beings, unlike machines, can make choices in their journey through life. However, they have no choice in their identity, makeup, or DNA. Machines are produced in volume, and the hope is that each one is identical, especially if the product is excellent. Cars, trucks, SUVs, trains, airplanes, and boats are all different, and within each group, there are additional differences, but all are modes of transportation.

Human beings are created, and each is different. Though they may be part of similar groups, all human beings are one group. The need to traverse between two or more points efficiently and effectively requires transportation. Disliking a mode of transportation is very different from disliking transportation overall.

It is one thing to dislike a person because of what they stand for. It is another thing entirely to hate someone simply because they are willing to take a stand.

Disliking or hating someone simply because they exist is very different from disliking them because they don't stand for what you do. This is defective detective detection.

Dislike what a person stands for, but do not dislike the person and hate the fact that they stand. We err when we dislike and reject people who simply stand as created, who stand for who they are when they have no choice in the matter.

The only acceptable rationale for collective groups being lumped together is regarding that which cannot be influenced. Lumping together based on the actions of one person, or even many people, is defective detective detection. Tying one person's error to a whole group of people is defective detective detection.

Discernment and viewing others as you would want to be viewed is the cure for discrimination and hatred at any level. We shouldn't let one person's actions define those who look like them and then apply the same rules to everyone within that group.

It is possible that there can be groups of people who all think, believe, or act the same. We hope for all to be lumped for good, but we often see lumping for bad. Good and bad are not determined by preference but can be seen in our eroding society. While grouping is possible, no two people are exactly the same. We are defective in our detection if we lump everyone into one group based on the actions of one, few, or even many.

The detective must make the distinction that is not defective by not lumping one, few, or many into a group. All may look similar, and one, few, or many may be like-minded, but this does not mean that *all* are like-minded. We must not fall into the trap of categorizing everyone based on our detection of one or even many. Doing so is defective.

Defective detective detection will poison any and everybody. The view is defective because the detective is flawed. How the detective sees one, few, or even many must not equate to how they see all.

What you see—the images pushed, promoted, discussed, and debated in the media—does not represent everyone. Do not fall into the trap of being defective in your detective work by believing what is convenient, promoted, and pushed out. If you do, you will be fooled into believing that all who look, think, and act alike are alike.

With such belief, our society continues to crumble—the result of defective detective detection.

59

PERCEPTIONS

SOMEONE SAYS, "YOU have a thing, and I want one too." What they are really saying is, "You have something that I don't. You have good things that suit you; I have some bad things, and they don't suit me."

With disparity and frustration there is a mutation: "You have something, and you are keeping me from having the same!" This mutation in perception has affected and plagued our society for a while now, and the ultimate outcome is a greater division between groups.

There are those who have things and are satisfied, and there are those who do not have and are not satisfied. The perceived reality is not that you have and others do not, but that you have and don't want others to have, so you keep them from attaining. They are not looking to obtain precisely what you have but to gain what suits them, just as you have what suits you, but for some of those who have, that is frightening.

The reality is that this is not merely a perception, but a reality.

—— 60 ——

BEFORE OUR EYES

ONE ADMINISTRATION STIRS up what society *denies.* The one that follows stirs up what society *hides.*

—— 61 ——

UNITY

A *HOUSE* (A PEOPLE, a society) divided against itself cannot and will not stand. However there is one thing we all agree on: we shall remain divided.

One group says, "We will promote different political parties, not to test and bring forward truth, but to divide."

Another says, "We will recognize differences among people, not to celebrate, learn, and stimulate thinking nor to search for and accept how those differences make up the whole. Rather, we remain committed to using those differences to divide."

There is one other item we agree on: we would rather go down divided than stand united.

Section 8

ROOTS OF DIVISION

A House Divided Cannot Stand

IT's A LOT easier to promise unity than deliver it, especially in a highly diverse population that is undergoing massive social, political, cultural, and technological change.

Politicians promise unity, business leaders create new technologies designed to bring us closer, and academics offer up fresh models of social engineering, yet we are more divided than ever. All of this makes finding solutions for complex problems difficult, if not impossible.

In this section, we will look at some of the root causes of division and what to do about it.

62

WHY? THAT'S A GOOD QUESTION

EVERYONE, REGARDLESS OF age, has asked a powerful question that almost always stems from a gaping need. Because it is so powerful and critical to the moment, this question often goes unanswered.

It has been and remains the question of the ages, applicable to virtually any situation, to any group, in any place, and under any circumstances. It is perhaps the most thoughtful and powerful question asked, and it is only one word, which may be what makes it so powerful.

The question is: Why?

Why? It is often asked to gain understanding. When we are perplexed, dumbfounded, or at our wits' end, when we see something that seems to have no good answer or explanation, we beg to know why. When what we see or experience does not seem to line up with what we think should be or with what was promised, expected, planned for, or experienced in the past, we find ourselves asking why.

Asking why becomes even more necessary when things seem irreconcilable, incongruent, or unjust. When there seems to be a bending or blurring of the truth, we ask why. When things are far Left, far Right, or just too far past the line of decorum, stretching society to a breaking point, we ask *why.*

Oddly, though, in many cases, we don't honestly want the answer to the question of why. When we have no good answer to *why* something happens, the question of why remains painfully unanswered. As a result, we are left perplexed, frustrated, jaded, and perhaps even infuriated because we don't know *why* it happened.

When our question is unanswered, we again ask why, searching for some sense of meaning. Over time we yearn for any response when there is silence to this straightforward question. In some cases, we no longer expect a good, reasonable response, as subconsciously, we suspect there is no good response. However, we may ask again to push for some irrefutable explanation, seeking a reasonable response that is defensible by its own standards and might stand the test of time.

The question of why something is the way it is often raises defenses and creates tension, hostility, and division, especially among children when this question is asked by their parents. Parents often find themselves asking this question, knowing the answer, and realizing that their kids don't know the answer or can't come up with a good answer. Parents often ask their children why as they try to get them to own up to their actions and take responsibility for the outcomes through deductive reasoning when possible.

Parents seldom ask why to learn from their children but to teach them. The parents hope that through discovery, their children will find the right answer—not the parent's answer but their own. Moreover, if the child does not offer the right answer, they must at least have a good answer. The response won't be accepted because it was offered but because it is based upon justifiable reason.

A simple example would be, "Why did you steal the cookie?" A good, answer would be, "I was hungry." There are many other answers a child could give: "I wanted the cookie." "I did not steal the cookie." "Everyone else had a cookie." "I needed a cookie." Perhaps some of these are good, but none is defensible.

Why is such a compelling, timely question that it commands, even demands, an attentive response. The irony is that as much as children do not, cannot, and should not be expected to know, they often ask why better than their parents because of this lack of knowledge. Parents ask why, thinking they know the answer. Children ask from a lack of knowledge.

In many cases, children have an internal radar. They ask why, not knowing what is right but simply recognizing something is wrong. They ask innocently, without agenda, bias, or expectation; they seek an explanation.

Children want to know how things work or why someone is saying one thing or another. They want to know why something is this or that way. They want to know why, and it is not enough for them to hear their parents say, "Because I said so," or, "That's just the way it is!"

Children often push adults, and if we cannot answer their question, they continue to ask in their innocent way. When we remain without an acceptable answer, adults will often attempt to dismiss the question, hoping due to their age and lack of knowledge, the children won't sniff us out.

In this scenario, we think we have lucked out with our answer. We hope the child may be too immature to know whether what we say is true. We exhale with relief if they cannot detect that we don't have a good answer. We think we can give a child a response that poo-poos them because they don't know any better.

Adults and children alike have doubts when things don't seem to add up. Even when we are trying to be dismissive, if we look carefully into the child's eyes, we can still see they are asking why. It's as if they are saying, "I hear and accept your answer as my parents, but I still don't know why. I hear you, but it still doesn't make sense."

We think that because children are more often naïve and inexperienced, they should just accept what adults say. This, sadly, is sometimes done as part of an agenda to poison the minds of children.

A child is just that: a child. They view and approach life in a childlike manner. As children, they cannot handle that which requires maturity and experience. This is why there is a legal age for driving, voting, drinking, and fighting in a war. (There was a time when we tried to protect children from others and themselves, predators within and without.)

A child asks why often because they are children who want to know what they cannot fully comprehend. It is valid to say childlike curiosity is wonderful. Children are teachable, and over time, they will accept what is being taught rather than resist. However, while they may not know exactly what is true, they know when something doesn't make sense. This is usually the reason they continue to ask why. Depending on who tires first, the child may say, "OK," which means, "I hear what you say, but it still makes no sense."

An adult will argue that this knowledge is not for a child and cannot be understood by an unformed and, possibly, uninformed mind. A child should not be expected to process things intended for adults or the mature. Sadly, while we know this to be true, we have erred in its application in the name of evolution and attaining higher learning. The adult will say, "Just accept it. You are a child; I am an adult. You cannot understand this, and it will only make sense when you grow up." Sadly, the adult will even say, "Trust me. I would never steer you wrong!"

Between the two responses, we find this truth: To a child, truth seems to always require further explanation to make sense. To an adult, truth seems to always require further explanation but never makes sense.

It is interesting that we find adults asking why more often than children do, even though we say it is the children who lack knowledge. The perplexing paradox is that children ask why to gain understanding while adults ask why to get an explanation. Both, however, demand a satisfactory answer. Otherwise, the unanswered question continues to be, *Why?*

The child trusts and accepts what you say when you get them to a place of understanding. An adult can bend the rules and even lie to a child if that adult has won the child's trust. When the truth the adult has altered makes sense to the child's understanding, they will accept it. This is great when the rules are bent to impart truth, but it is exceedingly dangerous when it is done to impart something false.

Partial truth, exaggeration, and half-truth will draw a why from a child. Sometimes, a child will ask why, get an answer, and still be perplexed, but will say, "OK?" The child is saying, "I hear what you are saying, and I understand the words, but not the bigger picture." In doing so, the child is not necessarily saying that it makes sense to them, but that they just hear you.

It does no one any good when the adult simply tries to explain away what the child cannot understand by bending the rules and saying, "That's just the way it is. You are too young to understand."

Our so-called progressive thinking requires explanation as it continues to change, and many voices are asking why. The one major challenge of a child accustomed to asking why regarding almost everything is that once things are explained, they change again and again. The child says, "It was explained once, and I thought I understood, but now it has changed again."

There is a difference between seeking understanding and seeking an explanation. Here is an interesting thought: Truth does not change, so it never needs further explanation. It only requires understanding.

Since "truth" continues to evolve, it is difficult to explain to a child. We silently tell ourselves as a society what a child can comprehend. We say, "A child is not expected to know that. You lack understanding because you are a child."

We blame the perplexing bewilderment on the child's inability to comprehend and accept the answer, giving little or no regard for the merit of the argument.

A child can distinguish between what is genuinely complex and what makes no sense, even if it is complex. Some will tell you everything it takes to get to the moon, requiring whiteboards, computers, and manuals to explain the process. In addition, others may simply say, "Get on the ship, buckle up, and enjoy the ride."

A child will remind you in the heat of the moment of the point, mission, or purpose no matter the time, circumstances, or situation. Adults get bogged down with details and things that they cannot control, while the child focuses on the destination.

A child pushes, asking why the journey is not getting him to the destination. "What you are saying, what you are doing, your explanation is not actually taking us where you say we are supposed to be going!"

A person will continue to ask why when ignored and even more so when not fully informed. This is apparent but not acknowledged. The person will wonder, "Do you know what you are saying?" This is especially true when the result of the matter proves to be an end unto itself, such as when someone says, "I am speaking out of belief, not necessarily truth!" Ignoring reality is not pragmatic, and such actions will take everything down.

Children tend to ask simple questions, don't they? We might even call their questions naïve. But are they?

The interesting fact is that as uninformed or naïve as they are, the questions the children ask are too often ones we, the mature, parents included, don't have answers for. We would be hard-pressed to have good, defensible answers.

There are answers to the *why* questions. However, those questions often go unanswered because the focus is not on the question but on trying to explain our answer.

Consider the *why* questions that continue to be asked. As mature adults, we should have an answer, but often we don't. We are trying to explain a question that, frankly, should not even have to be asked.

We must also be reminded that an answer to a question does not mean that one has to agree, but it does mean there is a sensible, defensible response. A mature child asking why is not looking for an answer. Instead, they want to know, "Why am I having to ask this question?"

Ask Your Mama

Why do males and females share the same facilities when there should or could be privacy and separation?

Why place males and females in situations that tempt their human desires?

Why put opposite sexes in settings that are ripe for inappropriate behavior?

Why have a male coach for an all-female team?

Why have a female coach for an all-male team?

Why send a female broadcaster into a male locker room?

Why send a male broadcaster into a female locker room?

Why send female soldiers to war, knowing that if captured, they will face horrors that some males have no remorse or conscience in committing?

Why are women fighting wars on foreign battlefields when they are needed on the battlefields of their homes?

Why do we allow males to decide at any moment that they feel like females and thus can go into women's bathrooms?

Why should males and females be in the same bathroom simultaneously?

Why safely transport children to their schools only to allow lies to be poured into their minds and souls under the guise of "higher learning"?

Why allow X-rated content into schools, where children are supposed to be safe?

Why allow teachers and others to speak lies into our children, to present complex topics that are years beyond their minds' ability to process?

Why allow anything the mind can conjure and the tongue can say to be disseminated—visually, audibly, and in print—to young minds, though they are unable to process what they are seeing, hearing, or reading?

Why allow uncontrolled distribution of content that has proven not to advance society?

Why, in the name of free speech, allow entertainment to destroy its consumers and producers?

Why should children with young, innocent, naïve, trusting minds have to listen to inappropriate content in the name of education?

Why are television and radio commercials that promote sex being broadcast during family programming that a parent wants to watch with their kids?

Why are most disclaimers and warnings about adult content simply an advance notice of them, with nothing restraining the content from being presented? *Why* use a warning instead of just not creating adult content in the first place?

Why does society hide the purpose of certain holidays?

Why does "anything goes" seem to be the norm?

Why are massages given by the opposite sex?

Why are there so many living on the streets, homeless and hungry, when there are people with billions of dollars?

A child asks: "*Why* do people curse but say I shouldn't do the same? *Why* do I see women with their bottoms exposed and men with their pants falling down when I keep being told to pull mine up? *Why* do I see two men or two women together as husband and husband and wife and wife? *Why* do people who don't look the same hate each other when I'm encouraged to get along with everyone (as much as possible)? *Why* do people who look different hate each other when at school everyone gets along? *Why* is the woman who feels like a man being treated the same way as someone born with a cleft palate, Down syndrome, or an inability to walk? *Why*, Mom? *Why* are people who feel a certain way being treated the same as people born a certain way? *Why*, Mom?"

A child asks too many questions that cannot be explained or that cannot be explained away. Many of the questions cannot be answered. Then there are some that can be explained, but mostly they are explained away.

That is the problem! The children are looking for understanding, and there is none, as much cannot be explained.

So the question remains, *Why*?

— 63 —

SHOCK VALUE

I T IS ERRANT to release content simply to spur conversation. Content that is described as shocking, compelling, or must-see, even if true, should not necessarily be produced, especially considering how vividly it can be presented with current technology.

The minds behind the writing, directing, and producing may have little to no values, scruples, or restraint. Much is done in the name of shock and freedom of speech that does little more than promote anarchy. The agenda, it would seem, is to dump the trash of society into people's minds.

The highest-grossing movies are rated G, and yet more non-G movies are produced.

As a society, we have marginalized life. The killing of human beings is so common we have designed video games that give points based on how many people can be eliminated. There is very little societal shock in the way we dramatize and even carry out the taking of lives, including through abortion.

There is one exception, one type of killing that humans can't seem to tolerate seeing: the crucifixion of Jesus!

— 64 —

FOCUS ON BLACK AND WHITE

W HITE TENDS TO show dirt. *Black* tends to hide dirt. *White* reveals. *Black* conceals. Both serve a purpose. Neither can be greater, better, or preferred over the other since they are equally important.

There has been so much pain, division, destruction, hate, and even death associated with the idea of black and white.

The two colors, though (if they could speak), have always begged the question, "Why be divided when together we complement and strengthen each other?"

Consider the pages you are reading at this very moment. If the print was black and the paper was black, nothing could be discerned—it would all be darkness. And if the print was white and the type was also, nothing could be discerned—it would only be a glare. The two are necessary and need each other for either to be seen.

Wouldn't it be wiser to celebrate the differences instead of using them as a point of division?

---- 65 ----

THE ASSIGNMENT: FULFILLED

You WILL BE called home when your assignment and purpose have been fulfilled on earth. You will be retired by death, which is the ceasing or conclusion of your purpose. Until that day, it is important to focus on fulfilling your purpose in the world.

When facing death, sickness, disease, hardship, or the impossible, know that your assignment in this world is not over until your purpose has been fulfilled. Jesus said, "It is finished," when He completed the tasks God had given to Him. Your purpose ends when you, too, can say, "It is finished!"

All too frequently, many people find themselves living without purpose.

As long as we have breath we have a purpose, and if we don't know what it is, then we should do our best to discover and fulfill it. It's only when we fulfill our purpose on planet Earth that we truly have a sense of accomplishment in our journey.

66

2C ONLY 2 COLORS IS NOT TO SEE

"Paint it all white," one said.

"This place needs some color to make it pop," said family and friends.

"Paint it all black," another said.

"This place needs some color to enhance it," said family and friends.

Fact: Neither black nor white are primary colors!

Depending on when you were born, you may recall the era when television shows and movies were only in black-and-white.

Those who didn't live during that period look back at black-and-white broadcasts wondering how anyone enjoyed them without the beauty of color. And today, with all our amazing technology, we have people taking full-color, high-resolution digital pictures and then rendering them black-and-white for publication.

It has to make you wonder, "Why all the fuss over those two colors?"

67

POWER AND RESPONSIBILITY

Those who hold positions in public office most often do so out of their desire for power. Yet they often forget that power is not given so they can serve themselves or control others but so they can serve others. To him who has much, much is expected, required, and demanded. With power comes *responsibility*. It is a burden and a privilege to manage, not a right to exploit.

They want to be great but directly oppose what defines greatness. As Martin Luther King Jr. said, "Anybody can be great because anybody can serve!"[1]

—— 68 ——

NUMB

Numbing your feelings by getting drunk seems great at the onset since it causes you to forget your troubles. However, there is something you cannot numb or simply forget, and that's the hangover that follows.

Alcohol is known to numb the senses as well as emotions. However, if not kept in check, it leaves us with a reputation of being depressed, angry, violent, or out of control. When this occurs, the hangover, or loss of a good name, is often worse than the reason we became numb in the first place.

While we may feel the need to block things out and ignore the realities of life, numbing ourselves, or putting our heads in the sand to avoid challenges, doesn't help. Eventually we dull our senses to the point where the end is worse than the beginning. If we deal with the real issue(s), we can usually avoid the hangover.

—— 69 ——

IT MAY FIT, BUT THAT DOESN'T MAKE IT RIGHT

If a truth supports and affirms my worldview, philosophy, social status, experiences, or feelings at any given moment, then it fits. I agree that this is truth. I will not accept that truth if it does not affirm and support what I believe.

It would seem that if it is truth, it is only for those to whom it fits.

We promote and accept all truth, but each person accepts their own truth because it fits their personal preferences.

We can all be *wrong*, but we cannot all be *right*!

— **70** —

ALL

SOME PEOPLE SAVE lives using a scalpel.

Some people save by protecting and defending our streets.

Some people save by providing an escape from reality, which we call entertainment.

Some people save by delivering goods.

Some people save by enabling technology.

Some people save by providing opportunities.

Some people save by helping the helpless.

Some people save by defending the defenseless.

Some people save by righting wrongs.

All people sacrifice, all can save, and therefore all are necessary.

— **71** —

VOTER FRAUD

PEOPLE, ESPECIALLY THOSE in Western society, talk about the right, privilege, and obligation to vote. Blood has been shed, countless sacrifices have been made, and some countries have even gained independence from securing the right to vote. It should never be taken lightly or for granted.

Therefore, you must vote for someone or something, it has been said. If you don't, something is wrong with you, and you don't deserve to be a citizen. If you don't vote, you can't complain or say *anything* about the conditions of society. People will say, "Keep your mouth shut because you did not vote!"

Question: What does one do when none of the choices offered is agreeable and worth voting for? What is one to do when the option is one of two terminal diseases? Is it better to vote for death by a bullet or a grenade?

Though one might be better because of its expediency, neither is desired. Normally in this simplistic proposition, the choice would be the quickest, least painful option. Remember this thought process the next time you are challenged with a choice. But be warned. If you use this reasoning, you likely will find yourself in a further dilemma: Do I go quickly, or should I get as much time as possible?

Of course, we would prefer to not vote for either option if both lead to death. But if we must choose, we will select the lesser evil. The distinction is that in neither case is one *voting for*! Voting *for* something is to essentially say, "I agree; I support; we are aligned in what we believe." It can also mean, "This is my preference—you have my vote of confidence."

Nowadays, using our definition of "casting a vote," voting for a particular candidate often is not a sign of alignment with that person. Instead, the vote cast is against the other option.

This is not always the case in our society. People acknowledge that they are voting for, supporting, and aligning with said candidate, whom they want to represent "their" collective cause.

There are two drivers when making decisions (casting votes), and when they are aligned, there is no personal conflict in mind and heart. You can have your heart set on something, but your head is elsewhere, or your mind agrees, but your heart is not in it. Neither one requires the other to function responsibly or with reason. They can actually be in opposition and still function.

It is with this paradigm that we often cast our votes. Oddly, we can cast a vote without our head or heart in the matter. A person can only *honestly* cast their vote using one of the two. When casting your vote, consider your mind and heart, but eliminate one. While it is possible the two can be aligned in one person, your heart and mind can rarely be aligned with another person's heart and mind as it relates to voting.

The exception to this hope is in the context of marriage, where the two become one. As it pertains to voting, there is, and perhaps should be, conflict.

In my heart, I desire peace; in my mind, I want money.

In my heart, I want to see unity; in my mind, I care only about certain people.

In my heart, I want the unknown left alone; in my mind, I want to be known.

In my heart, I know better, but my mind justifies things.

When we get it right, most of us vote with our minds, even if it is in conflict with our hearts. Some of us don't even vote with our minds. Almost none of us votes with our hearts, or if we say we do, it is offered that we should not be voting with our hearts.

The reasoning goes: "I am with you in my mind, but in my heart I will not die for you, and you will not die for me. I'm with you to a certain point."

It is best, and we are better as a society, when our minds are informed and aligned with our hearts, though most often that is not the case.

It is understandable to vote with our minds, though we may be conflicted. It is perplexing, though, when we *say* we vote with our hearts. Casting a vote of confidence intellectually is based on your desire that a particular person or candidate advance. Giving support is very different from casting a vote, as your support suggests the candidate agrees and is aligned with your heart.

Spoiler alert: those for whom you cast your vote care mostly for what you support with your mind and have little or no regard for your heart—who you are, what you value, or your standards.

It would be unprecedented and unreasonable to expect those you vote for to be aligned with your heart. This would imply that each heart and personal belief, being individual and different, can be known and in alignment.

Our votes mostly do not reflect where our hearts are but, more often, what our hearts are against. The heart is mostly excluded, and we vote primarily with our minds, and in doing so, we vote for what best suits us personally.

We arrive at the polling place and realize that we vote based on what suits us best, and it is our choice. We vote not because of an alignment of beliefs but based on the perceived expected personal benefit.

Consider the unspoken: "I am only voting for you because of what you say you will do for me. You are saying what I want to hear to get my vote. My heart is not with you, and your heart is not with me. I vote for you, but I do not choose you. You are not my choice."

Choice infers alignment, expectation, and support. Voting is often more an obligation, privilege, or requirement. In this regard, votes are cast with the mind as we pursue personal goals with obligation, privilege, and requirement mixed in, but it is rarely done by choice.

When this is realized, we see that our vote has little, if anything, to do with our heart; at best, it may have something to do with our head. Our vote only has meaning to us if it is aligned with our head or heart. Our vote can be aligned either with the heart or the head, but not likely with both.

In the context of political voting, the reality is that our head perceives what is better, and our heart senses what is bitter. We vote not based on choice and preference but on what is presented. Too often, it is the truest dilemma.

What is meaningful when considering the obligation and privilege of voting is whose ideology we most align with—who has our hearts? The seemingly perplexing but simple answer should be that no human, agency, party, organization, or institution is to have your heart. Why is this true? Thankfully, no human can truly know the heart of man. In fact, we cannot fully know and discern our own hearts.[1]

Can any person or political construct truly know your heart and deserve to have it? The better question is not whom you most align with but rather who most aligns with you.

Consider that most politicians seek their own agendas and purposes. They say they are for the people, but we discover they mean they are for certain people. History has shown that most politicians go into office one way, and yet end up governing and exiting sideways. What we voted for is not what we get.

Consider the words of past presidents:

- "Read my lips: no new taxes."[2]

- "I did not have sexual relations with that woman."[3]

- "That depends on what the meaning of 'is' is." [4]

- "I experimented with marijuana a time or two, and I didn't like it. I didn't inhale it."[5]

History has shown that a necessary attribute for being in politics is compromise. What follows is a change in character, leading to the pursuit of personal interests such as pet projects and paybacks to those who voted them into office. As a result, the slippery slope becomes a cliff.

Not everyone falls into political trappings, but the majority often does. A small minority is the exception. However, to participate, everyone must play in the mud. History has revealed that other professions play in the mud too. We find that people in medicine (e.g., Big Pharma), education, religion, nonprofit and for-profit organizations, and the arts and sciences may not have given their hearts, but they have sold or given their souls.

At the voting booth we find unity among those who are advancing their agenda and say they have our back. They are unified only in one aspect, and it is an individual benefit: each is seeking to gain your vote.

Voting for someone or something should not equate to that person having your heart. Following that thought process, you would never vote *for* but only *against* that which does not align with your heart. In doing so, you will have satisfied the voices who say you must vote because it is a privilege or obligation. Regardless of the outcome, you will have voted based on a rationale that makes sense, and not randomly, just to be doing something. Having used your mind instead of your heart, you will feel less heartburn.

Through all this, while your vote counts, it does not count for anything meaningful; it just counts. In recent years, the voting process has been so distorted by the very people in or running for office that there are times when a vote really does not count. In some cases, one vote conveniently counts as two.

Leaning into and upon truth, we find by looking to the best historical document ever written—the source of all truth—that God never voted. God never voted for people or elected anyone into a leadership position, but He did reject people.

If there is ever an opportunity for you to vote *for* someone, it would be only when you know their heart is *for* you.

No one can ever truly be for the people, as the people can never be totally one.

Spoiler alert: they can never be for you, as they can never know your heart, the same heart that even you cannot truly know.

In addition, it is almost impossible for you to know if their heart is truly for you or the people, as people's hearts change.

It is best to learn from God, and what we see is that He chose people. We learn that He chose by searching and finding those who could be trusted to make honest attempts to align with Him. Our vote of confidence should be for those aligned with God, not with themselves or us. His choice was and continues to be a man or woman after God's own heart!

We must realize that there is a difference between voting for someone and choosing someone. We vote for a person based on what is presented. We choose based on what is desired and sought. With this learning, we realize that we do not get to "choose" by selecting.

In this regard, our selection is made for us and given to us by others for whom we cast our vote. Given that we do not have a choice but must or should vote, what are we to do? What should one do with the privilege and responsibility of voting people into public office to serve as our leaders? Given that we cannot ultimately choose, as our choices are within the context of what is presented, we can follow the pattern of God. God rejected those presented before Him to choose from until He got to David, a man after His own heart.

Follow the pattern set by God. Reject the gangsters, who care only about themselves, and the drug dealers, who distribute things that cause people to become addicts. Reject those who look the part but whose hearts are not with you. Reject those who ignore and destroy or have no moral compass. Vote against them, the politicians who parade themselves for themselves. If there are only two options, vote *against* and never *for*. Choose the one closer to your values or reject the one who is furthest from your values, but never—no, never—vote *for* them.

Given that we cannot truly know a person's heart, we can only try to discern what they are saying. Most will try to say what people want to hear to get their votes. Having to choose among two or more evils, we are left to discern who wants our vote more.

The person who votes *for* will be the benefactor of what they voted for or supported. The person who rejects and casts a vote out of obligation, privilege, or expectation can expect a favorable outcome due to not voting for whatever it is. We all may suffer from a vote that we were not on board with, but those who did not vote for it suffer less. They may have headaches and heartaches but not heartburn, as they never had their heart in the matter to be burned.

Now, for those who would say, "This makes *no sense*; I will vote," then do so with a pure heart. Choose God and His ways. His options are just as flawed as we find ours to be, yet He accepts and rejects. God is looking to choose those who are aligned with Him, not those who *say* they are.

It matters little who you are aligned with, as they don't know you and often do not care. They just want your vote! It does not matter who is aligned with you, as they cannot know you and, therefore, can never truly care. This is the earthly way.

What is the answer to voter fraud? Vote using your mind, rejecting more than selecting. Let your heart determine if your mind is right.

72

CAPACITY IS HOLDING YOU

Is it possible to have too much capacity, too much ability, or too many possessions? Can you have so much that it actually is not capacity? Could you ever say, "My capacity has filled me to the point that I am empty? My capacity is weighing me down"?

The wealthy can do virtually anything at any time and go anywhere. The wealthy have been known to descend the fathoms of the seas, soar into and beyond the skies, and travel to virtually every land on earth.

The wealthy may say: "I can go anywhere I want; I just don't care to go *there* [to that neighborhood, community, or country]. I can go anywhere, but there are places I do not want to go, and I will not go. I am not being prevented by those who live there; it is because of what I have and who I am that I will not go to those places. Perhaps despite my capacity and resources, I do not have the capacity, or ability, to go anywhere.

"I can visit the deepest depths of the sea humans can tolerate and soar to the highest heights. Yet my capacity prevents me from visiting many places on earth, even places just around the corner.

"My capacity prevents me from experiencing so many things that are easily accessible. My capacity keeps me from benefiting from those who are different from me and from seeing how they benefit others and the world. My capacity is preventing me from experiencing my full capacity."

The poor have little capacity to do things or go places, and they might say, "I would like to go to [that neighborhood, community, country], but I am prevented." The wealthy, who can go anywhere, feel prevented because the location is undesirable. Meanwhile, the poor, who lack the capacity, are prevented from going even though the location is desirable. Which of the two are in bondage: the ones who are being denied by others or the ones who are denied by themselves?

History shows that more people overcame denials than those who did not. It seems society has progressed more thanks to people who did not have capacity than through the efforts of those who had capacity and succeeded without obstacles.

Progress is attainable when power is given to those who, being empty, have nothing to lose. They, having the capacity to be filled, have everything to gain. They can go anywhere and do anything, and with that power, they have the ability to make an impact everywhere.

73

MY ONLY RULE

JOHN MILTON'S NOVEL *Paradise Lost Book II* is as relevant today as ever. Every day in our world, countless people amplify the idea that it is better to rule in hell than to serve in heaven. They would rather do things their way than serve God's way.

74

TALK DIRTY TO ME

Talk dirty to me just one time each day.

Monday: "You are perfect; there is nothing defective or wrong with you."

Tuesday: "There is no truth."

Wednesday: "All roads lead to God!"

Thursday: "There is no God."

Friday: "No one tells me what to do."

Saturday: "Everyone has the right to do whatever they feel is right."

Sunday: "If it feels good, do it; it must be right."

Any day: "In keeping with progressive thinking, it is better to be covered with dirt than to be clean and exposed."

75

DIVISION

We divide and make distinctions over earthly things that perish. Juxtapose what we make distinctions about with why Jesus came, which was to unite us over things that do not perish, things that are heavenly and eternal.

Certain divisions are necessary and healthy. We must draw a line around what is right and wrong, what is true and false. Making distinctions and being divided over things with little value has always proven to be ineffective uses of energy and time.

Working toward that which lasts and brings people together is an excellent use of our time and energy.

There will be one last great division: those who destroy and promote destruction will be cast away from those who seek to protect life.

— 76 —

THE GOLDEN RULE

YOU HAVE PROBABLY heard it said that "he who owns the gold rules!" But who actually owns the gold? Moreover, who makes the rules? According to an ancient text:

> This is what the LORD Almighty says: "In a little while, I will once more shake the heavens and the earth, the sea and the dry land. I will shake all nations, and what is desired by all nations will come, and I will fill this house with glory," says the LORD Almighty. "The silver is mine and the gold is mine," declares the LORD Almighty. "The glory of this present house will be greater than the glory of the former house," says the LORD Almighty. "And in this place I will grant peace," declares the LORD Almighty.[1]

— 77 —

GLOBAL POLLUTION SHOULD
BE KEPT IN CHECK

MOST COUNTRIES DON'T want to consume what the US manufactures, so we produce little ourselves and rely upon others. Now manufacturing very little, we are dependent on others, who know we will consume anything, given that we don't produce much worth consuming ourselves!

When garbage is produced, unless one is a garbage collector, it is not accepted. No one wants or collects garbage. If, therefore, you are a producer of garbage, given that you are not wanted, you will cease operations. Now no longer a producer, you are in need of what others produce. They can send whatever, even garbage, and as a non-producer, whatever is sent is accepted.

When garbage is no longer consumed, it is no longer produced because there is no market for it and it becomes a burden to the ones who produce it in the first place. When we are no longer producers of what others will consume, we need what they produce. When we are accustomed to sending garbage to others because we no longer produce much ourselves, we are open to receiving and consuming the garbage of others, as well as our own. Eventually we become accustomed to trafficking in garbage.

When you no longer produce anything worth consuming, you become the consumer of anything, even goods from those who reject what you produce.

Countries are willing to send you goods they consider garbage, which you then will consume. When you fail to produce anything worth consuming, you fall prey to consuming anything sent.

78

THE REAL CRIME

No one is born a criminal. Criminals are created by the society and culture in which they live, rather than a biological or genetic outcome.

A society that does not promote justice and has a broken and perverted judicial system is a society that makes criminals. A crime of omission, of justice deprived and justice denied, births the crimes of commission.

This is the real crime.

— 79 —

WE THE PEOPLE

W E THE PEOPLE in the democratic society of the United States and the West focus more on who we *want* to lead than who *should* be leading.

We want our leaders to do what is best for us as individuals instead of what is best for us as a people, society, and nation.

To our leaders, "we the people" means "me the people." Because of this, there is much disparity and division, as our opinions are based on individual experiences.

We the people are divided, as are those whom we look to as guides, those elected to manage imputed power.

We the people, we all want or desire something. We the people are also our leaders—they also want or desire something.

We the people want leaders whose desire is to lead. We the people want them to be producers, as they demand us to be, and not consumers, which is what they say we are!

We the people want leaders who are not lacking or in need and therefore do not promote their own agendas.

We the people are asking for the unreasonable and unattainable from the people who say they are for the people.

We the people should be first asking, relying on, focusing on, and looking to the person who created us, the One who knows what we need, not the government. In doing so, we the people can rest in knowing that we will get what we need.

If we the people are bent on getting what we want by doing something other than asking the person who created us for His leadership, then we will get what we want—government, not the living God.

We the people should look away from governments that serve their own purposes and look to the One who puts governments in place to serve His purposes—by the people, for the people. Isaiah 9:6 says, "For to us a child is born, to us a son is given, and the government will be on his shoulders."

— 80 —

WHAT MATTERS

I't's not what you see at the time that matters most; it is what shows up later that truly matters! We call it an unintended consequence. It was unintended, but it happened, and that is what matters!

— 81 —

SOME THINGS WILL NEVER MAKE SENSE

There are things that, regardless of the times, will never make sense.

I once visited a hotel that positioned the toilet in such a way that no matter how you sat on it, the bathroom door would hit you. Additionally, you had to close the door to get to the toilet paper, which was situated behind the door. On top of all that misplacement, the seat was so low you would have thought it was meant for a two-year-old.

I asked myself who in their right mind would do this and why. At no time could this ever have made sense. In thinking about this, I realized some things make sense to us now that would not have made sense to us previously. Now we see the need for restraint or perhaps a need for decorum and respect when at one time it made sense to be less restrictive and let loose.

At one time, using chemicals such as mercury or lead seemed good because they were thought to be beneficial for healing and extending one's life. Over time, however, we have learned the opposite is true. Those chemicals are responsible for countless deaths, increased medical costs, and reduced quality of life. (We pray those who truly believed mercury and lead were beneficial and did not know about their negative effects.)

Then there are things such as the toilet placement that will never make sense. But the toilet does not have life-altering or life-ending implications.

Many things will never make sense. We would do well to recognize that and cease those practices.

— 82 —

TO GET CLEAN, YOU MUST GET DIRTY

In most cases, to get something clean, you must be willing to get dirty, as in the process of cleaning, one has to touch what is dirty.

When something needs to be cleaned, we often like to take the easy route and blow things off or away. We minimize the issue by blowing it off, and when we cannot do that, we try to blow it away. By blowing things off, we say, "It does not matter." By blowing things away, we are actually saying, "It might matter, but I don't care." Even if you don't care or think something does not matter, there is dirt, and sooner or later, it needs to be cleaned up.

If you are going to be the person who does the cleaning because you recognize something is dirty, then you must be willing to get down and dirty and let what you touch also touch you! Whatever is dirty almost always must be touched, if not directly then indirectly. Again, to clean something, you must be willing to get dirty.

There is a story told in which Jesus took His saliva, mixed it in the dirt, made mud, and put it on a blind man's eyes so he could see. Jesus got dirty to help the blind man, and the blind man had to be willing to get dirty to be healed. (I wonder if the blind man knew the mixture put on his eyes was made out of Jesus' saliva.)

There is another account where a man with leprosy had to dip himself into a dirty river seven times to be healed of his leprosy.

But the greatest example we can draw from is when Jesus descended from heaven to earth and became a servant.

Unlike many of us, Jesus did not consider being a servant a dead-end job. In fact, after close study, we can see that He chose by His actions to be known as a servant instead of as something loftier like a CEO or king. He came to address a need. Jesus willingly left heaven, which was perfection, and came to earth to touch the imperfect and unclean.

Jesus washed His disciples' feet. He got dirty. In fact, the Scriptures reveal that He took off His outer clothes, put a towel around Himself, and washed the disciples' feet with it. Jesus symbolically took upon Himself what was on them. He was willing to get dirty so they (and we) could be cleansed.

But while He was willing to get His hands dirty, He did not allow the dirt to make Him unclean. The dirt was on His garment, not Him! It is likely when He finished washing the disciples' feet, He removed the dirty garment. Again, He got dirty to make us clean.

The ills of society can be cured. We simply must be willing to get dirty.

83

THE COST OF PEACE

W E ARE UNWILLING to pay the cost of peace. People say they want peace but are not willing to do what it takes to attain peace.

"Better a dry crust with peace and quiet than a house full of feasting, with strife."[1]

The cost of peace is sacrifice and self-denial.

The benefit is life!

"A heart at peace gives life to the body but envy rots the bones."[2]

DOLLARS AND SENSE

Money Is a Great Servant but a Cruel Master

MANY PEOPLE BELIEVE money is the answer to all things and spend their lifetime chasing it. Unfortunately, money is a great servant but a cruel master.

In this section, we'll take a closer look at the ways money can be a servant or master in order to avoid becoming its slave.

84

IT'S ALWAYS ABOUT THE MONEY

People often say, "It's not about the money," but the truth is, it's always about the money.

Money is not only an important part of our lives, but it's also two-faced, and what we believe is true about money, and how we arrive at that conclusion, can be confusing.

Money Is Two-Faced

There are seven truths about the two faces of money that everyone who hopes to be successful needs to understand.

1. Money is loved if you have it, but hated if you lust after but don't have it.

2. Money can be held by anyone, but it is able to divide even the closest relationships.

3. Money is liked most when in a personal pocket but least when in another's pocket.

4. Money can rule a life if hoarded, but it can school the same person if ignored.

5. Money can buy what is seen but cannot possess what is unseen.

6. Money can fool you into rejecting "less is more," but it can make a fool out of you by robbing you with more.

7. Money can make you think you own it, but when loved, it owns you instead.

85

MONEY TALKS!

THE COMMON SAYING that "money talks" might be truer than what most people think. Consider the following.

I am money, and ...

I can be used, but I love to use those who use me.

I can get you to trust me as your security blanket.

I can get you to steal, lie, cheat, and even risk your very life just to have me.

I can change your character.

I can convince you that having more and more of me means you are a better human than those who do not have me.

I can convince you that in having me you make the rules.

I can empower you one day and destroy you the next.

I can lead you ...

I can lead you to use, put down, and keep people from attaining what you have or aspire to have.

I can lead you to believe that I am the be-all and end-all and worthy of you doing anything to obtain me.

I can lead you to use me to promote yourself, even at the expense of family, friends, and career.

I can lead you to believe that by having me, you are above the law.

I can lead you to believe in me more than God.

I can lead you to listen to me over common sense.

I can lead you to believe that you will never have enough.

I am a master illusionist—I can make you see what is not real or true ...

I cause those with much to think they have all they need and that they don't need anyone or anything else.

I can fill a person's heart and mind so there is no room for things such as faith.

I can convince you that you are more self-assured, worthy, and innately better when you have me.

I tell you that in having me, you are part of a uniquely worthy club, set apart and born to rule.

I can convince you that using others, even if it leads to the other person's demise, is how things should be. Moreover, when things are this way, you sleep well and say to yourself, "Well done."

I can lead you to believe you can never have enough.

I can convince you that always having more is what you want and you can only be satisfied by attaining more and more.

I can capture your imagination like a siren and put you under my spell.

I can put you into a delightful, drunken stupor that you would gladly remain in even though you know others also have been trapped by me.

I can fool you into believing there is no God by acting as and becoming your god.

I can make you …

I can make you think you possess me when I possess you.

I can make you think you have all you need by having me.

I can make you into someone you never thought you could be or wanted to become.

I can make you lose your integrity.

I can make you believe that by having me, you define what is right and the only wrongs in life are the bad things done to you.

I can make you change your values as you value me over your values.

I can make you trust in me more than God.

I can make you forfeit your soul when you trust in me.

Even as powerful as I am...
I cannot make you give to the poor.

I cannot make you sensitive and benevolent.

I cannot make you draw a line in the sand as to how much is enough.

I cannot make you do the things and make the decisions that would keep you from the hospital or save you from sickness.

I cannot save you from death.

I cannot bring you peace.

I cannot disarm myself; you must disarm me.

I cannot lie, but I don't always tell the truth.

I am everything and nothing ...
I am everything when it comes to selling your soul, and I am nothing when it comes to saving your soul.

I am money, and I have spoken.

Section 10

WISDOM

Right Is Right and Wrong Is Wrong

W E LIVE IN a time when a majority of people believe "right" is what they say it is and there is no outside, objective standard by which we are held accountable. My "right" is just as valid as your "right."

In this section, we will identify some of the earmarks and dangers of a culture based on moral and ethical relativism, and how to protect ourselves from the consequences.

86

POWER THE TORCH

THOSE WHO ARE innately gifted or paid to speak are *empowered*, whether journalists, athletes, entertainers, talk-show hosts, or anyone else in the public eye. It is this group of people who are added to the *haves*. They may not necessarily have great wealth or many possessions, but they are in positions to wield power. However, being in power does not ensure that power will be used for good. We must remember that being in power does not mean one deserves or is qualified to be in that position.

The *haves* are supposed to lead by serving, defending, and fighting for others. In times past, some entrusted with power took their call so seriously that they paid the ultimate price for justice. They gave their lives both figuratively and literally.

Considering the many perks entrusted to the *haves*, should not those enjoyments also be adjoined with an attitude of responsibility?

There is an outcome we desire to see from power being adjoined to responsibility. The *have-nots* and the *haves* both want, need, and embrace a common goal of justice.

An oversimplified and often misapplied definition of justice would be "getting what one deserves." This definition has meant different things to the *haves* and the *have-nots*. The *haves* would say, "We are getting and have gotten what we rightly deserve." The *have-nots* would say, "We are not getting and have not gotten what we rightly deserve." The *haves* would say justice, though not necessarily sought, has been served, while the *have-nots* would say justice has not been served. Both have a view of justice but experience it differently.

The unjust experience cannot be dismissed. The responsibility of those with possessions, platforms, and power will not go away.

When power is managed with justice, everyone enjoys safety, peace, and increased opportunities. With such outcomes, the *haves* no longer need to hide in their gated communities away from those who seek justice. Further, the *have-nots* will be free from the fears and hardships of not having. In fact, when they are the beneficiaries of justice, the *have-nots* will be inspired by the *haves* and be supportive of them.

When the *haves* champion justice, both the *haves* and *have-nots* will live peacefully and securely, as opportunity has been provided instead of prevented.

The enemy of justice is those who benefit from injustice and make it their goal to hoard possessions and control people, positions, and power for their benefit.

People who are born into power and use their status to justify unjust actions are major contributors to injustice. Their inheritance and position cause them to say, "Justice is served." With this mindset, many propagate injustice as a means to remain in power.

They empower those who prefer the thorns on the stem of the rose, thinking the thorns are necessary. "Keep the people oppressed, and you can control them," they say. "Give the people what they think they want, not what they need, and you will always have them under your control." They ask and answer the question, "Is it better to be loved or feared?" They know they are not loved!

The most responsible use of power is to take the torch and use it for its optimal purpose: to lead. A torch can be used to set things on fire or to guide the way. We shouldn't use the torch of empowerment to destroy people or ideas, but to build them up and lead the way.

Those in power are given the torch not to set fires but to lead the way to justice. They must fulfill that responsibility, lest that torch be removed and extinguished, and if that doesn't happen, it should, because that would be justice.

The torch in the right hands is a source of great hope.

However, if one cannot find the strength to lead yet abhors the alternative of setting fires that may burn one's own house, there is another option. The torch does not have to be extinguished. There is hope.

In a relay race, the team aims to win. If one person runs their leg of the race and the others fail to do so, the entire team will lose. Conversely, if one person runs poorly but hands off the baton to the next runner, there is hope for all to win.

If you won't lead, pass the torch to someone who will.

Don't set fires. Whatever you do, don't allow the torch of justice to be used for destructive purposes. In addition, don't allow it to be extinguished. If you can't or won't do this, pass the torch to someone who will. You will have done so to your benefit and perhaps fulfill your purpose as well.

CURING THE DISEASE OF DIS-EASE

I T HAS BEEN said, "The poor you will always have with you."[1] So too will we always have those who are up to no good and bent on doing wrong. However, the ability to eliminate, or at least slow, the disease of *dis-ease* is squarely on the shoulders of the *haves*.

To whom much is given, much is required, expected, and demanded. Yet the *haves* have not been in the business of eliminating *have-nots*. Rather, they create more poor and disadvantaged people by oppressing them, denying them justice and opportunities, and placing obstacles in their way.

Too frequently, when the *have-nots* finally have an opportunity in sight, it is snatched away by the *haves*.

THE DISEASE ...

Recall Charlie Brown and Lucy from the *Peanuts* cartoon. All Charlie Brown wanted to do was to kick the football so he could find fulfillment, have a sense of satisfaction, and feel equal with his peers. Lucy had power because she had the football, and no matter what the situation or circumstance, no matter how bad Charlie Brown felt, she could not resist the urge to place the football where he could see it, tell him he could kick it, and then pull it away.

Charlie Brown would line himself up, ready to kick the football. But after he had spent time running, thinking, planning, hoping, and believing, Lucy would snatch the football away and smile as Charlie Brown missed the kick and fell on his face. Then without missing a beat, she would say, "Charlie Brown, you blockhead!" Charlie Brown must have thought he was always a failure.

The Unshared Dis-Ease

Instead of freeing the *have-nots*, the *haves* keep them in captivity. In captivity, the *have-nots* most often are doomed to reproduce after themselves. The *have-nots* are born enslaved to a mindset but realize something is wrong. They recognize that they don't have and others do, and they become frustrated as a result. They say, "You keep showing me the football, and even if you don't let me see it, I know there is something more than not having. Each time I try to attain, it is not me that keeps me from having what I want or need, but you."

By and large, the *have-nots* would not resort to righting the wrongs and leveling the playing field by any means necessary, though if they tried this (as they have from time to time), they would not necessarily be criticized. It could be said that through denial, they have been forced by the *haves* into a lifestyle of wrongdoing, as they see illegal means as their only way to attain what the *haves* possess. This causes many law-abiding *have-nots* to be constantly mischaracterized as up to no good.

The number of *have-nots* is significantly greater than the number of *haves*. Still, both the *haves* and *have-nots* are capable of and engage in wrongdoing. They both have the same disease and are at dis-ease.

In fact, it is the *haves* who, though much fewer in number than the *have-nots*, do the largest-scale damage through their wrongdoing.

There is one key difference between the impact of the *haves* and *have-nots*. While both groups typically impact those with whom they directly engage, the *haves*' impact is often limited to the organizations they lead, while the *have-nots*' is limited to the communities where they live and the people they touch. The *have-nots*' scale is much larger, but it is influenced and set on fire by the *haves*.

It is dis-ease.

Disease

When a CEO or business leader is corrupt, the impact is largely contained to those within and connected to the organization the CEO influences. Most often, those affected, though jaded and even justifiably angry, are not changed by the corruption of the CEO. They normally would say, "I don't like what happened, and I hope justice is done so the culprit gets what they deserve."

When a group of *have-nots* becomes corporately corrupt, the impact is scaled to the size of their community and then the larger society. The *have-nots* simply say, "It was done to me, and now I will do it to others."

To those given much, much is expected, required, and demanded. The cure for our dis-ease, the pandemic that has plagued mankind for centuries, is found when those in power (the *haves*) rise to their purpose and reject temptations adjoined to possessing, which is equated with privilege. The cure for our dis-ease will come when the *haves* refuse to take advantage of the privilege of wealth.

The cure is found when the *haves* humbly accept that the power and influence they possess is a privilege that carries responsibility. When what is given, earned, or possessed does not live up to its innate purpose, it results in dis-ease.

The *haves* are not to hoard their possessions, keeping them for themselves or a select group who also have. To continue to have, one must release what they have so others can enjoy the same opportunities.

All too often, the *haves* say or think, "Why on earth would I want others to experience what I have?" They rationalize by saying, "Why should I divulge secrets with those who work less so they can share in my success, which they have not earned? Why should they enjoy the fruits of my labor when they haven't paid the price and gone through what I and those who preceded me have gone through?"

As different as the *haves* and *have-nots* are, they share this in common: both desire to pursue their purpose for being. The difference between the two is that when denied the opportunity to attain what they seek, the *haves* already have something while the *have-nots* do not. Having things with little opportunity is much different from having nothing with no opportunity. Having things but feeling as though you are lacking is the same as having nothing and feeling you are lacking.

When there is a lack, regardless of how much you do or do not have, eventually the fruit of those unmet needs will come knocking, taking a variety of forms. Hunger, crime, homelessness, inflation, the need for increased security and jails, abortion, scams, and cybercrimes represent the short list. Most people, the *haves* and *have-nots* alike, will not understand this, as it is a suppressed truth. Lack is not good for anyone.

One person's disease of dis-ease should not become my dis-ease. I should not feel bad so someone else can feel good. However, if there is to be a disease of dis-ease, the cure falls on the shoulders of the *haves*. The *haves'* dis-ease is in getting more and having their way, while the *have-nots'* dis-ease is in being denied the chance to simply get and never being able to have their own way.

The cure for the disease of dis-ease—the purpose of privilege—is to promote opportunity for everyone regardless of status, ethnicity, gender, and so on. To him who has, much is expected, required, and demanded. With much power comes much responsibility.

DESPERATE

THE OPPRESSED SAY, "I'm suffocating. I'm being denied and am desperate for a breath of equal human opportunity."

Being denied opportunity causes desperation and shapes the desperate. Desperate people do desperate things, which are not always the best things.

RIGHTING THE WRONGS

THE WRONGS OF society cannot be made right if you simply give back and don't help people gain the skills needed to manage the gift. Disease (or dis-ease) requires curing, not covering.

Giving loans to those who have been historically denied them through oppression has proven unsuccessful in helping people build wealth when the same people aren't given the opportunity to gain the skill set or *capacity* needed to repay the loan. In fact, when we do this, we do more harm than if we had done nothing. Giving for the sake of giving fails, and its failure should be recognized as counterproductive to righting wrongs.

This may explain why we find governments at odds with the private sector. Governments prefer to offer loans to garner votes; the private sector prefers to withhold opportunity to garner profits. The government and private sector—the *haves*—do this at the expense of the *have-nots*, which ultimately will lead to society's demise.

This approach is opposite the one Jesus took. He made it a point to feed both the mind and the body.

Section 11

GOVERNMENT

We May Be Lost, but There Is Always a Lifeline

WE COMPLAIN ABOUT the way our government functions but rarely admit that we are responsible for it. Whether we admit it or not, "we the people" still have the power to vote.

In this section, we will look at how we got here and why we shouldn't be surprised by the state of affairs, whether good, bad, or ugly.

90

GOVERNMENT FOR THE PEOPLE

THE POWER BROKERS, those in power, the lawmakers say: "The rules we make are for the people to live by, not us! We passed those laws to govern the people, not ourselves!"

91

COVID-19, 2020

DID YOU NOTICE in the year 2020 that the tools that influence and shape what and how we see our society (movies, television, news programming, and social media) were having record-high ratings that were trending higher? Then suddenly in the year 2020, they all got shut down.

See clearly with 20/20 vision.

NEW WINE

The One Who Makes the Rules
Knows the Outcome

ALTHOUGH WE ARE living in the most advanced time in human history, we can't seem to resolve the most basic societal ills: poverty, hunger, bigotry, war, racism, injustice, and even genocide.

In this section, we will look at some common challenges facing our modern world and time-tested, proven answers.

—————————— 92 ——————————

NEW WINE

To KNOW TRUTH, we must return to the beginning, to the most reliable resource known to mankind. With no skin in the game, I sought the oldest collection of writings, the ones that have stood the test of time, the best-selling, most challenged book of all time.

The book I refer to has been debated, reviled, said to be rubbish, and even ignored as not worthy of respect. Taking on all who would rise against it, it has survived all challengers and challenges.

To those who have embraced, trusted, and relied upon it, this book has been of great benefit, serving as a guide, a plumb line, a rock. To those who have challenged its writings and rejected it, this book has been viewed as foolish. It has spoken to generations past and has proven its ability to thrive through future generations.

People use the term *common sense*. However, look around, and it's easy to see that sense is often not common. This book considers the common and makes sense of it. It is apparent we lack common and good sense. Too many of us just share our opinions and are unwilling to consider others' points of view.

We, therefore, must look to a guide in our discussions and debates about truth. We look around and see and experience many things and then say, "This doesn't make sense." One could also say, "This makes *no sense*." There is a subtle difference between the two. Regarding the first, most would agree that our experiences and where we have landed as a society do not make sense. The latter offers that our experiences and where we have landed as a society result from not knowing the truth. Both propositions agree that sense is lacking.

Sense isn't necessarily what makes sense to you or me but rather what has been proven throughout time to be true. The sense founded in this book does not require belief or even fact.

The sense presented in this best-selling book does not require faith, as it stands alone in support of itself and is self-validated. The sense founded in this book does not require belief in it; it needs no outside support, as it can stand any test because it is the truth.

This sense is superior to facts. Facts are not necessarily truth and do not always reflect truth. For the learned and those in the know, consider a few facts: numbers never lie, but they don't always tell the truth! Consider that what was factual in the past is no longer factual because of new knowledge and techniques. What happened to Pluto? It was the ninth planet in our solar system, then it was reclassified. Facts change; truth does not! Sense can be found in the book of truth. There are many truths, but collectively they are all truth; they are not in opposition.

There is only one set of truths to be found, and it is found and validated in the book that sells more than 100 million copies each year and been translated into at least 690 languages.[1] An estimated five billion copies are in print, dwarfing the next closest book, which has only 800 million copies in print.[2]

Do the math: with 100 million copies sold each year and more than five billion copies in print, this book has withstood the test of time, making it both self-validated and externally validated.

The book that I refer to is the one that lets you *know sense*, the one that has withstood scrutiny and debate—not from one source but from multitudes of critics and haters, spanning life's entire spectrum. Scientists, scholars, lawyers, theologians, and those who would argue its authenticity have all failed to destroy, minimize, or effectively distort what this book proclaims.

This book has proven itself worthy of being referenced and relied upon in any situation, and it is a guide. It can be trusted as the foundation that never changes. This book can be used as the plumb line when clarity is needed. This book, unlike any other, is always stable, always reliable, and always trustworthy as being true.

This book has been and remains the specific source of life to countless people and has been the portal that saves humanity from death.

In this book the truth is revealed; it no longer needs to be discovered or found. This book and the truth it reveals require only the slightest bit of sense, an open mind, and a desire to know sense.

This book is remarkable, especially when you consider it has more than forty authors who wrote over many years, lived at different times, and were not able to share information as easily as we do now. They had no social media, no collaboration, no reference checks, and no research to refer to.

This book's mission continues to be validated. It effectively uses its power to influence, change, and impact lives favorably, as this book is the truth.

Thankfully, this book does not hide, apologize, or dumb down thoughts but is overt rather than covert in presenting truth. This book reveals but also conceals; it protects but also exposes. This book does not deny the truth because it cannot deny itself. This book's diverse authors represent the truth without apology.

Over their collective lifetimes, the authors of this book experienced much travail, change, hardship, objection, hate, and at times unbelief. And yet, through it all, their accounts are in harmonious agreement and communicate the same message.

One author complements the other. Each author offers building blocks with limitless options for how you can navigate, and all lead to the same end. No matter what order you assemble the writings, there is no wrong way to read, as you will gain knowledge and be exposed to truth.

You can read the book in part, allowing each component to stand alone, which they do so eloquently and beautifully, or it can be read in its entirety so the link among the parts is evident. This is because each contribution was inspired by the same source, the Author of all that is truth!

This book I look to and ask you to examine is more than a resource but the source of truth. Suffice it to say, this book defends itself and does not need anyone to prove it is a reliable, worthy work of literature. Thus, from this point, the text itself will be presented to bring these pages to a close. With new wine, we can *know sense*.

———————— 93 ————————

GIVE THE PEOPLE WHAT THEY WANT!

In the past, people asked for a king to lead them; today, they seek a president to show them the way. "Give us a leader we can see instead of God, whom we cannot see." Then and now, God is rejected, though not overtly. We don't say outright, "I reject God," but we say subtly, "Give us what we want, not what we need. Give us *who* we want!"

Our rejection of God is partly due to our reliance on things seen; we are moved or impressed by what can be seen with physical eyes. We tend to allow physical appearance to influence our choices.

Secondly, we tend to prefer what man offers versus what God says and promises. When the people rejected God in ancient times and asked for a king, God told them what to expect. Most of what He said the king would do was not favorable to the very people who wanted him.

Despite the bad report, they said, "When can he start!?" So it is in our current times. We don't want God. We want a president to rule, just like the other nations. We would rather have man tell and inform us than God!

If the people don't want the rule of God, He'll give the people what they want, even to their detriment.

Remember this: you may get what you want, but God still will have His way!

———————— 94 ————————

A CHOICE PRO-CREATION

Genesis 5:1–2 says, "This [is] an account of the births of Adam: In the day of God's preparing man, in the likeness of God He hath made him; a male and a female He hath prepared them, and He blesseth them, and calleth their name Man, in the day of their being prepared" (YLT).

This is the written account of Adam's family line. When God created mankind, He made them in His likeness.

> So God created mankind in his own image, in the image of God he created them; male and female he created them. God blessed them and said to them, "Be fruitful and increase in number; fill the earth and subdue it."
>
> —GENESIS 1:27–28

God's plan was to unite male and female, to make them one flesh, and this intent is revealed in their design. God's plan, the one He intended us to experience, is that the two would dwell together and function as one though they are two.

> That is why a man leaves his father and mother and is united to his wife, and they become one flesh.
>
> —GENESIS 2:24

God has given us His desire, direction, and choice. Man, made in His image, has been given free will and can make choices. But the choices we made reflect man, not God. The choices reflect a fallen image, not the image of God.

The pro-choice position is effectively anti-life and directly pro-death. Choosing lifestyles that cannot procreate and deciding to terminate or abort life are applauded as pro-choice.

The pro-life position opposes most of the choices made by those who call themselves pro-choice. The pro-choice position makes the selection that opposes pro-life. If it didn't, there would be no need to emphasis the "right" to choose. Being "pro-choice" was developed in the mind of man!

The pro-life position comes from the mind of God. He made us male and female, reflecting His image and resulting in procreation and the propagation of life.

One position offers life with no option for death; the other offers a choice of life or death, and most often death is chosen.

The two are similar but, thankfully, very different.

Know sense.

—— 95 ——

DEI–WHO CARES?

GOD CARES AND has more to say about diversity, equity, and inclusion (DEI) than we will ever know. Here is what He has to say on the matter. Revelation 5:9 says, "And they sang a new song, saying: 'You are worthy to take the scroll and to open its seals, because you were slain, and with your blood you purchased for God persons from every tribe and language and people and nation.'"

Jesus died for every tribe, language, people, and nation, though we just call it all "race." Not only did He die for all, but He purchased those who will accept Him. He died so all the very different people made in His image would be included in the family of God!

Effective DEI polices must be driven from the top down, which we have failed to do. However, we have a great example to draw from to inform us. We see perfectly the top-down principle, noticing that God Himself invited everyone made in His image to be part of His family; they simply must accept His invitation.

Following is the best DEI policy and vision, with its supporting, undeniable, vetted, time-tested, undisputed, self-evident truths that answer the whys of the policy.

THE TRUE WHY BEHIND DEI

There are different kinds of service, but the same Lord. There are different kinds of working, but in all of them and in everyone it is the same God at work. Now to each one the manifestation of the Spirit is given for the common good. To one there is given through the Spirit a message of wisdom, to another a message of knowledge by means of the same Spirit, to another faith by the same Spirit, to another gifts of healing by that one Spirit, to another miraculous powers, to another prophecy, to another distinguishing between spirits, to another speaking in different kinds of tongues, and to still another the interpretation of tongues.

All these are the work of one and the same Spirit, and he distributes them to each one, just as he determines. Just as a body, though one, has many parts, but all its many parts form one body, so it is with Christ. For we were all baptized by one Spirit so as to form one body—whether Jews or Gentiles, slave or free—and we were all given the one Spirit to drink. Even so the body is not made up of one part but of many.

—1 Corinthians 12:5–14

The True Why Behind DEI Disability Policy

Now if the foot should say, "Because I am not a hand, I do not belong to the body," it would not for that reason stop being part the body. And if the ear should say, "Because I am not an eye, I do not belong to the body," it would not for that reason stop being part of the body. If the whole body were an eye, where would the sense of hearing be? If the whole body were an ear, where would the sense of smell be?

But in fact God has placed the parts in the body, every one of them, just as he wanted them to be. If they were all one part, where would the body be? As it is, there are many parts, but one body. The eye cannot say to the hand, "I don't need you!" And the head cannot say to the feet, "I don't need you!" On the contrary, those parts of the body that seem to be weaker are indispensable, and the parts that we think are less honorable we treat with special honor. And the parts that are unpresentable are treated with special modesty, while our presentable parts need no special treatment.

But God has put the body together, giving greater honor to the parts that lacked it, so that there should be no division in the body, but that its parts should have equal concern for each other. If one part suffers, every part suffers with it; if one part is honored, every part rejoices with it.

—1 Corinthians 12:15–26

The True Why Behind DEI
Disability Policy Practice

> But God chose the foolish things of the world to shame the wise; God chose the weak things of the world to shame the strong. God chose the lowly things of this world and the despised things—and the things that are not—to nullify the things that are, so that no one may boast before him.
>
> —1 Corinthians 1:27–29

God's ways are almost always countercultural and unconventional, but they have always proved to be the best and most effective.

We need not look for or figure out a good DEI policy when there is already one written that has proven to be the best!

— 96 —

DEALING WITH DIVERSITY

Our way of dealing with diversity falls short! Increased policies, new laws, expanded definitions, meetings, workshops, diversity ombudsmen, and various organizations are part of a seemingly endless list that is failing the test.

Jesus offers a radical way of dealing with diversity—love.

> A new command I give you: Love one another. As I have loved you, so you must love one another. By this everyone will know that you are my disciples, if you love one another.
>
> —John 13:34–35

> My command is this: Love each other as I have loved you. Greater love has no one than this: to lay down one's life for one's friends. You are my friends if you do what I command.
>
> —John 15:12–14

97

RIGHT BUT EXECUTED WRONG

THE DECLARATION OF Independence was aligned with God's Word. Still, something went wrong, possibly at its inception or in its application.

"We hold these truths to be self-evident, that all men are created equal, that they are endowed by their Creator with certain unalienable Rights, that among these are Life, Liberty and the pursuit of Happiness," the Declaration of Independence states.

Long before the Declaration of Independence, which was perhaps influenced by Scripture, Jesus held the following truths to be self-evident: that all men are created equal and are endowed by their Creator with certain unalienable rights. He said:

> Just as the Father knows me and I know the Father—and I lay down my life for the sheep. *I have other sheep that are not of this sheep pen. I must bring them also.* They too will listen to my voice, and there shall be one flock and one shepherd.
>
> —JOHN 10:15–16, EMPHASIS ADDED

98

I LOVE YOU?

WE TALK ABOUT love almost daily, and we easily say, "I love you." But do we know the real meaning of love?

> This is how we know what love is: Jesus Christ laid down his life for us. And we ought to lay down our lives for our brothers and sisters. If anyone has material possessions and sees a brother or sister in need but has no pity on them, how can the

love of God be in that person? Dear children, let us not love with words or speech but with actions and in truth.

—1 JOHN 3:16–18

99

SUBJECT SUBJECTED

NO ONE GETS to determine who has too much or too little when subject to Him. We do get to determine how much we need and if we are still in need.

No one would argue that there is a significant difference between a want and a need, and yet unmet needs get heaven's attention.

> And when they measured it by the owner, the one who gathered much did not have too much, and the one who gathered little did not have too little. Everyone had gathered just as much as they needed.
>
> —EXODUS 16:18

When you are submitted to Him, your wants also are submitted to Him, and you ask only for what you need.

> Two things I ask of you, LORD; do not refuse me before I die: keep falsehood and lies far from me; give me neither poverty nor riches, *but give me only my daily bread.* Otherwise, I may have too much and disown you and say, "Who is the LORD?" Or I may become poor and steal, and so dishonor the name of my God.
>
> —PROVERBS 30:7–9, EMPHASIS ADDED

The writer asks for only what is needed: "Give me only my daily bread." Having what one needs is what we all desire, aspire to, and require. Attaining what one wants is a blessing in life but not a necessity.

When subject to Him, we take only what we need. When subjected to Him, we look to the needs of others!

All of us can have what we want when we all have what we need!

100

BUZZER ALERTS WRONG

ONE PERSON SAYS: "I don't like you; you are not like me. I don't like what you stand for, sit for, or believe. I don't like how you think, where you live, what you look like, or what you do. Basically, I don't like you. I don't care for how you speak, what you look like, how you do what you do, where you've been, or who you hang with. Actually, it's not just that I don't like you—I hate you!

"I hate you for good reason, but I know I am saved because of my deeds. I have served in my church for years in different capacities. I have influenced many people. I am respected in my community. I give to the poor. I tithe. I do all of this and more because I love God."

Know Sense tells us, "Whoever claims to love God yet hates a brother or sister is a liar. For whoever does not love their brother and sister, whom they have seen, cannot love God, whom they have not seen."[1]

101

THE QUESTION CLARIFIED

THE QUESTION: "WHAT must I do to inherit eternal life?" Jesus answered: Love God *and* your neighbor. In loving God, you will love your neighbor. Another way of saying it is, "You cannot say you love God if you do not love your neighbor."

One of them, an expert in the law, tested him with this question: "Teacher, which is the greatest commandment in the

Law?" Jesus replied: "'Love the Lord your God with all your heart and with all your soul and with all your mind.' This is the first and greatest commandment. And the second is like it: 'Love your neighbor as yourself.'"

—MATTHEW 22:35–39

Notably, most people have little problem *professing* their love for God. Still, most people have a problem *understanding* who their neighbor is. Jesus clears up any confusion regarding the matter. He addresses the question of what one must do to inherit eternal life and ties it to what one must do in this life!

THE QUESTION CLARIFIED ...

On one occasion an expert in the law stood up to test Jesus. "Teacher," he asked, "what must I do to inherit eternal life?"

"What is written in the Law?" he replied. "How do you read it?"

He answered, "'Love the Lord your God with all your heart and with all your soul and with all your strength and with all your mind'; and, 'Love your neighbor as yourself.'"

"You have answered correctly," Jesus replied. "Do this and you will live."

But he wanted to justify himself, so he asked Jesus, "And who is my neighbor?"

In reply Jesus said: "A man was going down from Jerusalem to Jericho, when he was attacked by robbers. They stripped him of his clothes, beat him and went away, leaving him half dead. A priest happened to be going down the same road, and when he saw the man, he passed by on the other side. So too, a Levite, when he came to the place and saw him, passed by on the other side. But a Samaritan, as he traveled, came where the man was; and when he saw him, he took pity on him. He went to him and bandaged his wounds, pouring on oil and wine. Then he put the man on his own donkey, brought him to an inn and took care of him. The next day he took out two denarii[c] and gave them to the innkeeper. 'Look after him,' he said, 'and when I return, I will reimburse you for any extra expense you may have.'

"Which of these three do you think was a neighbor to the man who fell into the hands of robbers?"

The expert in the law replied, "The one who had mercy on him."

Jesus told him, "Go and do likewise."

—LUKE 10:25–37

—————— 102 ——————

FORGET THE PHONE– ANSWER THE CALL!

A BLUEPRINT FOR CHANGE has been given to those who say, "I love God, I serve Him, and my truth and confidence are in Him!" Change is specific to those whom God has called to be His agents or ambassadors of change. We who are called by His name have received the best and most important call we will ever get!

The LORD appeared to him at night and said: "I have heard your prayer and have chosen this place for myself as a temple for sacrifices. When I shut up the heavens so that there is no rain, or command locusts to devour the land or send a plague among my people, if my people, who are called by my name, will humble themselves and pray and seek my face and turn from their wicked ways, then I will hear from heaven, and I will forgive their sin and will heal their land. Now my eyes will be open and my ears attentive to the prayers offered in this place. I have chosen and consecrated this temple so that my Name may be there forever. My eyes and my heart will always be there."

—2 CHRONICLES 7:12–16

The world (and your world) will change when those called by His name humble themselves, pray, seek His face, and turn from their wicked ways. Change is dependent on those who are called.

103

THE BEST PARTNER EVER

DOING THINGS OR flying alone is not good (as it is not good that man dwells alone). In business or life, a partner—someone who can assist you, someone you can lean and rely on, a partner who cares the way you care and cares for you—would be a wonderful find.

God wants to be our partner. We allow Him to do so when we do what is necessary for Him to come alongside us. We need Him as our partner, and He offers to be! He does not need us to be His partner. We benefit when we invite Him and His presence by building our lives according to what He tells us to do.

> Then have them make a sanctuary for me, and I will dwell among them. Make this tabernacle and all its furnishings exactly like the pattern I will show you.
>
> —EXODUS 25:8–9

104

INJUSTICE, NO PEACE;
JUSTICE, KNOW PEACE

WHEN WE KNOW sense, we are confronted with and denounce injustice by embracing and promoting what justice really is!

INJUSTICE ...

"Shout it aloud, do not hold back. Raise your voice like a trumpet. Declare to my people their rebellion and to the descendants of Jacob their sins. For day after day they seek me out; they seem eager to know my ways, as if they were a nation that does what is right and has not forsaken the commands of its God. They ask me for just decisions and seem eager for God to come near them. 'Why have we fasted,' they say, 'and you have not seen it? Why have we humbled ourselves, and you have not noticed?'

"Yet on the day of your fasting, you do as you please and exploit all your workers. Your fasting ends in quarreling and strife, and in striking each other with wicked fists. You cannot fast as you do today and expect your voice to be heard on high. Is this the kind of fast I have chosen, only a day for people to humble themselves? Is it only for bowing one's head like a reed and for lying in sackcloth and ashes? Is that what you call a fast, a day acceptable to the LORD?"

—ISAIAH 58:1–5

JUSTICE ...

"Is not this the kind of fasting I have chosen: to loose the chains of injustice and untie the cords of the yoke, to set the oppressed free and break every yoke? Is it not to share your food with the hungry and to provide the poor wanderer with shelter—when you see the naked, to clothe them, and not to turn away from your own flesh and blood? Then your light will break forth like the dawn, and your healing will quickly appear; then your righteousness will go before you, and the glory of the LORD will be your rear guard. Then you will call, and the LORD will answer; you will cry for help, and he will say: Here am I. If you do away with the yoke of oppression, with the pointing finger and malicious talk, and if you spend yourselves in behalf of the hungry and satisfy the needs of the oppressed, then your light will rise in the darkness, and your night will become like the noonday."

—ISAIAH 58:6–10

PEACE AS A RESULT OF JUSTICE ...

"The LORD will guide you always; he will satisfy your needs in a sun-scorched land and will strengthen your frame. You will be like a well-watered garden, like a spring whose waters never fail. Your people will rebuild the ancient ruins and will raise up the age-old foundations; you will be called Repairer of Broken Walls, Restorer of Streets with Dwellings. If you keep your feet from breaking the Sabbath and from doing as you please on my holy day, if you call the Sabbath a delight and the LORD's holy day honorable, and if you honor it by not going your own way and not doing as you please or speaking idle words, then you will find your joy in the LORD, and I will cause you to ride in triumph on the heights of the land and to feast on the inheritance of your father Jacob." For the mouth of the LORD has spoken.

—ISAIAH 58:11–14

105

DIFFERENCES? THERE IS ONLY ONE!

HOW DID JESUS address the differences among people, which we call race? How did He address racism? His way makes no *earthly* sense. First, He came for the sick, not the healthy, and people who choose to focus on the differences among people are not healthy, although they likely do not know or will not admit it. This group of people—like the religious, the self-righteous, and those with great possessions—often say by their actions and lifestyles, "I don't need Jesus."

They ask, "Who are you to tell me how to live? Who are you to judge me? No one tells me what to do." They are sick. However, while Jesus came for the sick and not the healthy, certain sick people desired to remain as they were, as they were more comfortable that way.

This condition and why Jesus does not heal them is explained in Matthew 13:15: "For this people's heart has become calloused; they hardly hear with their ears, and they have closed their eyes. Otherwise they might see with their eyes, hear with their ears, understand with their hearts and turn, and I would heal them."

As imperfect as we know we are, we have almost perfectly missed the mark in the way we treat one another. Too often, we don't treat others as equals all made in God's image.

One of the major issues Jesus came to earth to address was man-made differences, issues that continue to plague society. These man-made differences have resulted in wars, division, endless debates, poverty, slavery, sex trafficking—the list seems endless.

He first demonstrated that regardless of condition, all are equal, as all are made in God's image and all are offered salvation. Whosoever will accept and believe in Him shall be saved.[1] He established that all people are worth dying for and worth saving.

While Jesus addressed the sinfulness of our conduct and character by dying in our place, He would not dismiss the differences we have used to divide us. He proclaimed that He made all people differently and that all are equally valuable. We are all one in Him.

He came for the sick and will heal all who accept His offer. The one and only distinction Jesus would make is between those who respond to His invitation and those who do not!

He would specifically differentiate between the sick and the healthy, the blind and those who say they can see, the wheat and the weeds, the saved and the lost, and those with faith and those without. The great difference between each group was who their father was: God or the devil. In fact, Jesus would ask, "Who is your father?" Or He would tell certain people who their father was based on their actions.

Who a person puts their faith in is what distinguishes one group from another, and this is the only distinction Jesus made. He was patient with those with little to no faith and did not group them with those who would deny or oppose Him.

As much as Jesus spoke of oneness and the power therein, He also did not dodge spelling out this significant difference. In one sense, it could be said that Jesus is the most discriminating of all.

Jesus spoke of how hard it is for the rich—the *haves*—to enter the kingdom of heaven in Mark 10:23. And Jesus spoke of the poor—the *have-nots*—in Matthew 26:11, saying they will always be with us. Jesus pointed out differences and made distinctions.

Yet while Jesus acknowledged differences, those differences were not rooted in the people themselves but in their condition. The differences were not based on how they were born but in how they were made by society, what they had fallen into through their actions, or what God had called them to so He would be glorified.

We can find no statements where Jesus related the human condition to their image, as mankind was made in the image of God. Man's condition was based on *their* choice to disregard God's direction, and this distinction continues even today.

A major difference between man and God is how we make distinctions. God makes distinctions based on obedience and disobedience, righteousness and unrighteousness, and so on. Man's distinctions typically stem from selfish reasons. Men and women leverage differences for one's benefit and another's demise. This is a result of our flawed humanity and selfish ambitions.

What did Jesus do when He came across a person who was different, such as a Samaritan, a widow, a leper, a person who was blind, or one who could not find their way? He first acknowledged that their actions revealed their need—that they were not healthy but sick. Then He would make another distinction and relate mankind's often misguided choices to their intent.

While Jesus made distinctions, pointed out differences, and was discriminating, His actions and statements were not designed to separate or divide. He would, however, point out that mankind's ungodly actions resulted in separation and division. Jesus ultimately would leave the dividing to the Father.

It has been noted that Jesus treated people differently, acknowledged man-made distinctions, and addressed each person based on their condition and need.

Jesus addressed the proper, God-given order in marriage and family. In doing so, He ensured we understood that order does not negate or eliminate equality between men and women. In fact, He would ensure that we understood that equality is God's order.

In John 4, Jesus met a woman with a sordid history who had been married several times. She was busy getting water to satisfy her current need. She was different from Jesus because she was a Samaritan, a fact she brought up because it was unusual for a Jewish person like Jesus to talk with a Samaritan like her. We would label the way the Samaritans were treated as racism.

Jesus' initial response was to go to the real issue and address her need, not to discuss their differences. The distinction He made was regarding her actions and who had her heart. He told her, "You Samaritans worship what you do not know; we, the Jews, worship what we do know."[2]

The distinction Jesus made—*know sense*—was not in the people but in their actions. As all people are the same, only their actions differentiate them.

Because we are made in God's image, we have been empowered to make judgments. Neglecting to do so, we fail in our responsibility to differentiate between right and wrong, good and bad. While we are to make judgments, those judgments are only to be directed toward people's actions, not the people themselves. Equally important is that we do not judge whole groups of people who look the same based on the actions of one. There are always outliers and exceptions. Even within a group that appears to be the same, people may act the same, but this is almost always because of how they have been treated, not because of the way they were born.

There was an occasion when Jesus said, "I was sent only to the lost sheep of Israel."[3] Yet we found Him healing *all* who were oppressed—Jew, Greek, Samaritan, Roman, and so on.[4]

Jesus often encountered those who did not think they needed Him like the Pharisees, Sadducees, and teachers of the Law who were just as lost. Being lost, they did not see themselves as in need or as doing the will of the devil. Jesus made distinctions based on choices, so He reminded them, "You are of your father the devil because you do what he does."[5]

Again, His one distinction was based on who they were following, not who they were as people made in His image. And while Jesus was always open to them changing, repenting, and reaching out, He treated them differently based on their actions and choices.

The one difference we can make is between the saved and unsaved, lost and found, believers and unbelievers! This difference is strategic, as we are to seek those who are not following God and share the message of salvation with them.

While Jesus acknowledged and made distinctions, He offered only one difference that resulted in two distinctions: whether you serve God or the devil. Distinctions such as skin color, background, geography, or even physical anatomy (male or female) reflect God's greatness and are equally great.

Jesus said He came first for the lost sheep of Israel but later said He had other sheep to add to the fold.[6] All are equal.

Know sense: The man-made issues of racial equality and systemic racism have never been issues of Scripture. Our Lord never needed to deal with them because in the beginning God said, "Let *us* make mankind in our image, in our likeness."[7] The Godhead is One but is expressed as Three. We too are all made from One but individually express God's creativity. There are many different groups, but we are all made in the image of God. One race of people with many differences cannot have racism, as there is only one race.

The conclusion to the matter of difference is in 1 John 4:20: "Whoever claims to love God yet hates a brother or sister is a liar. For whoever does not love their brother and sister, whom they have seen, cannot love God, whom they have not seen."

Know sense: It is not true to say you love God, who you don't see, if you don't love the people made in His image whom you can see! When you love someone made in God's image who looks different from you, that love gets God's attention.

106

I WANT TO BE FIRST

THE INTERESTING THING about order is that we want to be first only when it is good or advantageous. Yet being first does not always determine one's treatment. If you are first to receive, then you also are first to have an expectation of what you should receive.

Jesus came first to God's chosen people—the Jewish people, the Israelites. There are others who also are considered the first fruits—those who would come to believe in Him!

107

HIS EYE, YOUR I

REVELATION: "I HAVE considered how I see myself and others, but I have not considered how He sees me. "
A revelation from the Book of Revelation:

"To the angel of the church in Laodicea write:

These are the words of the Amen, the faithful and true witness, the ruler of God's creation. I know your deeds, that you are neither cold nor hot. I wish you were either one or the other! So, because you are lukewarm—neither hot nor cold—I am about to spit you out of my mouth. You say, 'I am rich; I have acquired wealth and do not need a thing.' But you do not realize that you are wretched, pitiful, poor, blind and naked. I counsel you to buy from me gold refined in the fire, so you can become rich; and white clothes to wear, so you can cover your shameful nakedness; and salve to put on your eyes, so you can see.

Those whom I love I rebuke and discipline. So be earnest and repent. Here I am! I stand at the door and knock. If anyone

hears my voice and opens the door, I will come in and eat with
that person, and they with me.

To the one who is victorious, I will give the right to sit with
me on my throne, just as I was victorious and sat down with
my Father on his throne. Whoever has ears, let them hear what
the Spirit says to the churches."

—Revelation 3:14–22

108

RIGHTING THE RIGHT

Righting the right, is that a mistype? Not so! What we normally
hear is righting the wrong. However, what we need is to right the
right. This "right" is not political. Rather, it refers to those who have been
given rights. The need is to right those who have been given rights. It
should be repeated that these rights have been given, not earned, or even
deserved.

Why, one may ask, are rights given to people? Regardless of how or
why rights are given, they either test or tempt the recipient. Whether they
are tests or (less likely) temptations, rights always carry a responsibility. If
they are tests, your character will be proven. If they are temptations, your
character will be tried. When a person passes the test and their character
has been tried by fire, purified, and perfected, they then need only to be
proven by not yielding to temptation. The proof in this regard is living up
to the responsibility the rights bring.

THE TRUE UP

The phrase *righting the right* is akin to the term *true up*. It means to make
something true, equal, or correct.

The first right is God showing Himself and His ways as being right. He
owns everything, especially what we need—and we all have needs—and
with this comes a commitment to meet those needs. God does not leave
our needs unmet. Considering that God does not need to be righted, He

models the responsibility shared by everyone who has rights by addressing the needs of mankind. We have needs, and because God not only loves us but also possess what we need, He met our needs. This is evident in one of the best-known verses in the Bible, John 3:16: "For God so loved the world that he gave his one and only Son, that whoever believes in him shall not perish but have eternal life."

John 3:16 demonstrates the spiritual values those who have rights are to follow—namely, sacrificing oneself or that which is precious for the benefit of others. Then there is a demonstration of the natural. In righting the right, God sets those who have as an example and causes them to do what is right to those who have not. As an example, consider the Israelites, who were enslaved in Egypt. The Egyptians reflect those who have, and the Israelites are examples of those who are without or in bondage.

God is righting the right as it relates to having possessions and money and using them for self while others are suffering or going without. Perhaps more egregious is when the suffering or lack is caused by those who have the ability to provide relief.

In the scenario to follow, God is righting those to whom He has given rights.

It is those with possessions and responsibility—the *haves*—who are being tested. And we must be reminded that along with any test, temptation lurks. As mentioned previously, we are tested to determine if we will be true and not give in to temptation or fulfill our obligation.

We are tested from above by God and tempted from below by ourselves.

It's Always About the Money ...

God set the events in order and said, "Shall I tell Abraham what I am going to do?"[1]

For 430 years, the people of Israel were enslaved in Egypt. The entire time—before, during, and after—God had a plan. The people were sent to Egypt for a purpose, and in the end, God would be glorified by righting the wrongs of the right—the people originally given possessions and/or power. The *haves* had an opportunity to bless others, but they chose to abuse what they were given.

Reflecting the depravity of mankind, the *haves* don't seem to be satisfied just to have. It appears their greatest satisfaction comes when they have material things and others do not!

Thankfully, God cares deeply for His people, particularly those who have been deprived of their rights. When those made in His image—those who have been chosen and called by His name—experience injustice, God gets on the move to right the right.

Injustice, misuse, and abuse of what has been given are so serious to God that He made a covenant with Himself to right the right. We read:

> Abram brought all these to him, cut them in two and arranged the halves opposite each other; the birds, however, he did not cut in half. Then birds of prey came down on the carcasses, but Abram drove them away. As the sun was setting, Abram fell into a deep sleep, and a thick and dreadful darkness came over him. Then the LORD said to him, "Know for certain that for four hundred years your descendants will be strangers in a country not their own and that they will be enslaved and mistreated there. But I will punish the nation they serve as slaves, and afterward they will come out with great possessions. You, however, will go to your ancestors in peace and be buried at a good old age."
>
> —GENESIS 15:10–15

God established a covenant between Himself and mankind. His covenant brings Him glory when there is justice. His justice is to help the helpless, the weak, the poor, those who have been dealt a bad hand, the disenfranchised, the elderly, the disabled, the widows, the throwaways of our society, the downcast, those oppressed by the devil, and the unfortunate. And that is the short list. He is the defender of anyone who has been or is being denied what God intended for those made in His image.

People are not meant to be in bondage. When God sees people in bondage, He seeks to set them free. God's first desire is to use those on earth who will do the right thing as He instructs. If those who have been given rights on the earth do not respond to God's call, then God will intervene from heaven to right the right.

It should be noted that when God says that He Himself is going to intervene to free the oppressed, His intervention is direct. He brings events to deal with injustices. Through the events He orchestrates, He invites us to respond rightly to injustice.

God sees that those with rights need to be righted because they have not lived up to the responsibility they have been given, so He intervenes and rights the right.

> The LORD said, "I have indeed seen the misery of my people in Egypt. I have heard them crying out because of their slave drivers, and I am concerned about their suffering. So I have come down to rescue them from the hand of the Egyptians and to bring them up out of that land into a good and spacious land, a land flowing with milk and honey."
>
> —Exodus 3:7–8

God's intent is always to work through man, and that remains His goal. Our most impactful experiences, the ones through which we realize the greatest level of tangible satisfaction, almost always are connected to our five physical senses: sight, hearing, touch, taste, and smell.

While God often does things without human agents, He is intentional about using that which we naturally sense.

He moves to right those who have—those who are in the wrong by hoarding and oppressing others—and works the situation together to benefit those who have been wronged. God is saying, "What I have given you is not for you to hoard but to use to benefit others." In righting the right, He provides the test to see whether they will bow to the temptation to ignore His command and hoard.

> [God said], "And now the cry of the Israelites has reached me, and I have seen the way the Egyptians are oppressing them. So now, go. I am sending you to Pharaoh to bring my people the Israelites out of Egypt."
>
> —Exodus 3:9–10

We, mankind, will reject anyone trying to right the right, so God must right the right. This is what He did when the Israelites were enslaved in

Egypt. He said, "I am going down Myself to rescue My people." He used trouble to deliver His people out of trouble, just as He foretold.

> So I will stretch out my hand and strike the Egyptians with all the wonders that I will perform among them. After that, he will let you go. And I will make the Egyptians favorably disposed toward this people, so that when you leave you will not go empty-handed. Every woman is to ask her neighbor and any woman living in her house for articles of silver and gold and for clothing, which you will put on your sons and daughters. And so you will plunder the Egyptians.
>
> —Exodus 3:20–22

There is good news for all. God will right the right—He will true everything up! He will make things true, equal, or correct.

There are questions for those who need to be trued up: Are you willing to be trued up? Are you willing to be righted? You have been given much but are not right in your dealings. Are you willing to allow God to right your wrongs by righting your rights?

If you do not do what is right with that which has been given to you, then I Am has the right to do what you should, and I Am shall!

At the Exodus, God fulfilled His promise. He righted the right, causing the *haves* to demonstrate justice to the *have-nots*.

> Now the LORD had said to Moses, "I will bring one more plague on Pharaoh and on Egypt. After that, he will let you go from here, and when he does, he will drive you out completely. Tell the people that men and women alike are to ask their neighbors for articles of silver and gold." (The LORD made the Egyptians favorably disposed toward the people, and Moses himself was highly regarded in Egypt by Pharaoh's officials and by the people.)
>
> —Exodus 11:1–3

In righting the right, it's always about the money. Not so, says God, but God knows man.

The *haves* are meant to help the *have-nots*. The *haves* have not just been given the right to have; they also have a responsibility. Regardless of how their wealth was attained—whether earned or gifted—the *haves* have rights that also come with a responsibility to do justice. If the *haves* do not act justly, eventually God will.

There is a lot to do. People are perishing, and there is no justice. When there is no justice from the hands of man, God will right the right. We see God righting the right in Exodus 12.

> The Egyptians urged the people to hurry and leave the country. "For otherwise," they said, "we will all die!" So the people took their dough before the yeast was added, and carried it on their shoulders in kneading troughs wrapped in clothing. The Israelites did as Moses instructed and asked the Egyptians for articles of silver and gold and for clothing. The LORD had made the Egyptians favorably disposed toward the people, and they gave them what they asked for; so they plundered the Egyptians.
>
> —EXODUS 12: 33–36

After all was said and done, the Israelites were set free, but they didn't leave Egypt empty-handed. God's way is justice—righting the wrong by righting the right, letting the oppressed go free but not empty-handed. He made the right—those who had been called to do what is right to those who were in need—do what was right. When you are in need, it is right for you to expect those who have to address the needs of those who have not. One day you may be helping someone in need.

Those who have must give to those who have not out of what has been given to them. This is why they have been given what they possess. Blessings continue as those who have material goods give to those in need.

When God rights the right, everything is right! This is the most significant need: to right the right.

—————— **109** ——————

WHAT GOD WANTS FOR YOU

I have seen a grievous evil under the sun: wealth hoarded to the harm of its owners.

—Ecclesiastes 5:13

God gives some people wealth, possessions and honor, so that they lack nothing their hearts desire, but God does not grant them the ability to enjoy them, and strangers enjoy them instead. This is meaningless, a grievous evil.

—Ecclesiastes 6:2

And when they measured it by the owner, the one who gathered much did not have too much, and the one who gathered little did not have too little. Everyone had gathered just as much as they needed.

—Exodus 16:18

Command those who are rich in this present world not to be arrogant nor to put their hope in wealth, which is so uncertain, but to put their hope in God, who richly provides us with everything for our enjoyment. Command them to do good, to be rich in good deeds, and to be generous and willing to share. In this way they will lay up treasure for themselves as a firm foundation for the coming age, so that they may take hold of the life that is truly life.

—1 Timothy 6:17–19

God wants little from you but *much* for you!

— 110 —

NET WORTH

THIS IS THE great deception: that what we have defines our worth, value, status, and position in life. The thinking is that if you have much in this world—toys, accolades, and friends—you must be important and valuable.

You do the math and surmise that whoever has the greatest total should be on top. The reverse applies as well—whoever has the least in this world's eyes is worth less.

In God's kingdom economy, it is not what we have but the One who made us in His image that defines our worth.

You were worth dying for!

— 111 —

AS IT IS IN HEAVEN BUT NOT ON EARTH

THE MINDSET OF many in the church and business world is that you can enjoy the benefits of knowing Christ in heaven but not here on earth. "As it is in heaven but not here on earth"—we don't say this, but we live it!

Christians who have achieved success will share Christ with others because He says to do so. But sharing secrets of success to help others attain the additional blessings—we are not all feeling that.

"Every good gift and every perfect gift is from above, and comes down from the Father."[1]

A SEQUEL THAT'S BETTER THAN THE ORIGINAL!

PERHAPS THE CURSE of success is the need to repeat past performances. You have a hit song that tops the charts, and now there is an expectation to repeat that success. The first movie is great, so the second is expected to be just as good or better.

Once you have one success, it is expected that you will have another. This is the weight of expectations.

Follow-ups or sequels rarely meet expectations. Sequels are usually not better than the original, and many times they are not even comparable to their predecessors. Interestingly, those who get to do a sequel often find themselves overacting in an attempt to live up to or surpass the original. Attempts to live up to or improve on the original fail so often that such expectations should not be considered reasonable.

Sequels rarely surpass the original. But there has been one extreme exception. The only performance in history that eclipsed the original—so much so that the original serves it—was Jesus coming to earth.

In the beginning, there was darkness. God called light into being. Mankind fell, and in His love, God provided His laws to protect and save us after the fall. As good as those laws were, we proved we could not obey them. Therefore, God Himself came by sending His Son, who would keep His laws for us. We need only believe in Him, and in doing so, we can be saved through Him.

The original covenant, as good and glorious as it is, is now overshadowed by the sequel.

113

THE TIME IS NOW

THE BOOK OF Proverbs is a source of wisdom. Such a statement invites us to lean in as the time will come when knowledge surpasses wisdom. The time is now!

The foundation of wisdom is the fear of the Lord!

The reason for rejecting this wisdom is simple: one does not fear the Lord.

The time is now!

We know much, do much, and do so absent of wisdom.

The time is now!

"We have evolved," we say.

"We have progressed," we say.

We have added letters to a seemingly endless bucket of "come as you desire" and "whosoever will" acronyms in the name of progressive knowledge.

The time is now!

We have the knowledge to do many things. We do many things that can be termed great; however, most things we do have not made us or our society great!

The time is now!

We have the knowledge to abort a person before birth and harvest their body parts.

The time is now!

We can change or alter the naturally designed, appointed anatomy given at birth.

The time is now!

We rely on our knowledge—which is finite and changes as we learn, discover, and evolve—and give no regard to infinite knowledge to know all.

The time is now!

The book of wisdom also speaks to knowledge, but it is a different knowledge from what we seek in our day.

The time is now!

Our knowledge lacks understanding because we do not fear the Lord.

The time is now!

Knowledge has surpassed wisdom, as there is no fear of God.

The time is now!

"The fear of the LORD is the beginning of wisdom, knowledge of the Holy One is understanding."[1]

The time is now!

114

BLESSED AND HIGHLY FAVORED!

BEING BLESSED AND highly favored does not equate to not having to go through the undesired.

Being blessed and highly favored guarantees an ultimate beneficial outcome, even in situations we prefer to avoid.

115

PRO-CHOICE

CHOICE—DESTROY THE NATURAL before it can take shape or be born, or alter that which has already been born.

The first choice is termed abortion. Perhaps the end goal or underlying aim of abortion is to destroy the person before they can fully form. The pro-choice position provides an option for how they would be naturally born. Abortion is even offered as a choice when doctors, in all their wisdom and knowledge, predict imperfections. The choice to abort the life is suggested, if not highly recommended.

To make this action palatable socially and to our consciences, we have redefined and confused birth so that abortion is not called murder. As we know, in every society, the termination of a life after birth is murder. So we say that life has not begun, creating new definitions to avoid calling it murder.

Pro-choice—if we cannot abort or commit murder, the second choice we make is based on how we feel. We proclaim we were born in the wrong body, and we then choose to alter ourselves based on how we feel.

For the agnostics, atheists, religious, and non-religious, there is, perhaps, an unknown truth. Whether you believe in God, God is pro-choice.

Deuteronomy 30:19 says, "This day I call the heavens and the earth as witnesses against you that I have set before you life and death, blessings and curses. Now choose life, so that you and your children may live."

When life seems to provide options (some people, thankfully, don't see abortion as an option), follow the rule of God. We have been given options and choices by God. He is pro-choice, and He says, "Choose life!"

—————————— **116** ——————————

WHAT WAS SAID WON'T BE SAID

*W*HAT WAS SAID *that won't be said*: we have been warned that due to culture or current evolution of society, these things common in the world will reap God's wrath.

—————————— **117** ——————————

THE BEST BET

*T*HE PROBLEM WITH gambling is that you are taking a chance and risking what you have or value in hopes of getting more. You place a wager, hoping or expecting a return that exceeds what you put at risk.

We are now a society raised and conditioned to gamble. We are a culture of gamblers that takes risks and lives based on random chance.

Taking risks should be applauded. Taking risks in the context of chance should be avoided. Every day people gamble their futures, putting their lives at risk.

The best gamble is not to gamble but to put your wager on that which is predictable and proven.

The best gamble is no gamble: "Salvation is found in no one else, for there is no other name under heaven given to mankind by which we must be saved."[1]

— 118 —

WHOSE IMAGE?

V IRTUALLY EVERY CULTURE that believes in Jesus has a picture or an image of Jesus that reflects them. None presents a picture or image of them reflecting Him.

— 119 —

THE END OF THE MATTER

C ANCEL CULTURE IS really counter culture, or you could call it "cancel human," since it is people who are being canceled.

Mankind was made in the image of God (Genesis 1:27), and all of mankind came from one man and woman (Genesis 5:1–2). The only difference or distinction was male and female. No colors or other physical attributes are mentioned as distinctive, as all skin colors and physical attributes make up mankind.

Mankind represents perhaps the greatest diversity ever seen on earth. From one man came male and female with almost limitless or endless representations, not by selection or election (choice) but by birth (creation).

While we are diverse and different, three commonalties are shared among all people. We all have been made in God's image (Genesis 1:27), we all have a date with death (Hebrews 9:27), and we all have a sin nature and have sinned (Romans 3:23; 7:17–18).

We share a fourth but different commonality. As different and diverse as we are, we are extended an invitation and opportunity to escape the death resulting from sin.

Regardless of where one may have been born, what one looks like, what one possesses or lacks, all have been given a way out of the clutches of death. All have been given the option and opportunity to escape death (Romans 1:20).

God's plan for mankind, made in His image—both those who would say they had no choice and those who would say they were born one way but not the way they feel—is that we would not perish but be saved (2 Peter 3:9).

The problem has been seen, the purpose of salvation has been stated, and what remains is His plan, the end of the matter.

Salvation from sin and death came first to the Jews and then to the rest of the world (John 4:22). God's choice is that He selects the least, little, and overlooked. Jesus was born a Jew and preached the good news to His people, but He said He had other sheep to bring into the fold (John 10:16), making way for all people to be redeemed.

Jesus' disciple Peter recognized this truth and preached this message.

> Then Peter began to speak: "I now realize how true it is that God does not show favoritism but accepts from every nation the one who fears him and does what is right. You know the message God sent to the people of Israel, announcing the good news of peace through Jesus Christ, who is Lord of all. You know what has happened throughout the province of Judea, beginning in Galilee after the baptism that John preached—how God anointed Jesus of Nazareth with the Holy Spirit and power, and how he went around doing good and healing all who were under the power of the devil, because God was with him.
>
> "We are witnesses of everything he did in the country of the Jews and in Jerusalem. They killed him by hanging him

on a cross, but God raised him from the dead on the third day and caused him to be seen. He was not seen by all the people, but by witnesses whom God had already chosen—by us who ate and drank with him after he rose from the dead. He commanded us to preach to the people and to testify that he is the one whom God appointed as judge of the living and the dead. All the prophets testify about him that everyone who believes in him receives forgiveness of sins through his name."

—ACTS 10:34–43

Paul, too, echoed what Jesus established, preaching equality and salvation for all. We all are equal and should be treated as such.

There is neither Jew nor Gentile, neither slave nor free, nor is there male and female, for you are all one in Christ Jesus. If you belong to Christ, then you are Abraham's seed, and heirs according to the promise.

—GALATIANS 3:28–29

Jesus came full of grace and truth to undo what mankind has done.

Cancel human

Everyone born is made in God's image and thus are all equal and should be treated as such. Our own undoing is that we have not treated one another as equals.

One of the primary and most overlooked, underappreciated characteristics of God is that He is liberal. God gives freely to whom He chooses, not because of them but because of Him! His choice, though, is tied to those who are called by His name and qualified by responding to His call. He gives freely to all who are called by His name and made in His image. The message, the invitation to come, shows that we all are equal, and He gives us equal opportunity. Made in His image, we should do the same to others.

The apostle Paul speaks of equality in the context of salvation and related actions:

> Our desire is not that others might be relieved while you are
> hard pressed, but that there might be equality. At the present
> time your plenty will supply what they need, so that in turn
> their plenty will supply what you need. The goal is equality,
> as it is written: "The one who gathered much did not have too
> much, and the one who gathered little did not have too little."
>
> —2 Corinthians 8:13–15

We are to share the gospel freely (John 3:16) and do so through the things He gives (Matthew 25:31–45; 1 John 3:17–18).

Judgment begins in the household of God. God has freely given to us, and He expects us to freely give to others (Matthew 10:7–8).

Revelation 5:9 informs us that there are people "from every tribe and language and people and nation" around the throne of God. Jesus worked overtime to eliminate man-made discrimination by praying we would be one. But He also realized there would be those made in His image who would reject Him (John 1:11; John 17:11).

God ultimately makes only two distinctions among people: those whose names are written in the Book of Life and those whose names are not.

Jesus further explains how to distinguish those made in His image. During His time on the earth, Jesus distinguished between those who served God and those who served the devil, those whose Father is God and those whose father is the devil, those who obey and those who disobey, and those who believe and those who do not believe. The qualifier is not what one says but what one does and how one lives (John 8:44; Matthew 13; Matthew 25:31).

In Revelation 5:9, we see representative distinctions made—people "from every tribe and language and people and nation" around the throne of God. These groups are very different, representing just a glimmer of God's vastness, yet they are the same because there is no discrimination among those who have been saved.

Jesus was discriminating and discerning based upon actions, mainly pertaining to those made in His image loving one another.

God's standards are as follows:

> If anyone has material possessions and sees a brother or sister
> in need but has no pity on them, how can the love of God be
> in that person? Dear children, let us not love with words or
> speech but with actions and in truth.
>
> —1 John 3:17–18

This brings great clarity to the question of who we are to love (who is our brother and sister). It is not what the person looks like that matters but the fact that he or she can be seen.

> Whoever claims to love God yet hates a brother or sister is a
> liar. For whoever does not love their brother and sister, whom
> they have seen, cannot love God, whom they have not seen.
>
> —1 John 4:20

There is a solution to the world's problems of cancel culture, or cancel human. The cure for most of society's ills has been given through a distinct group of people: the people of God. God calls His people the called, chosen, elect. Those who have accepted His gift of salvation, those who are called by His name, are His people.

In Scripture, we find whom God looks to move through and use to bring notice to who is in control:

> When I shut up the heavens so that there is no rain, or
> command locusts to devour the land or send a plague among
> my people, if my people, who are called by my name, will
> humble themselves and pray and seek my face and turn from
> their wicked ways, then I will hear from heaven, and I will
> forgive their sin and will heal their land.
>
> —2 Chronicles 7:13–14

The called, the chosen, the elect—those who responded to His call— carry the blessed benefit of a burden that is not burdensome. The called, chosen, and elect need not concern themselves with the overall responsibility or the end of the matter. Those who are called need only avail themselves to be used by God so He can accomplish His purposes. The called are to do so without discriminating among mankind—cancel culture, or cancel human—because God has already established the only distinctions we are to live by. Those called by His name have been given standards to live by, and one of those standards is to reach the unsaved.

Cancel culture > cancel human

While God has made the two distinctions, they were made after His purpose. In the beginning of all things, God said, "Let us make mankind in our image, in our likeness" (Genesis 1:26). Cancel culture aside, God loves those made in His image (John 3:16).

THE TRUTH OF THE MATTER

We ask, "Who is the Lord that I should listen or obey Him?" This question was asked long before any of us was born. In Exodus 5:2, "Pharaoh said, 'Who is the LORD, that I should obey him and let Israel go? I do not know the LORD and I will not let Israel go.'"

In our present day and age, we ask, "What is truth?" having said there is no truth. Again, there is nothing new in the question, as such was asked well before any of us was born.

> You are a king, then!" said Pilate.
>
> Jesus answered, "You say that I am a king. In fact, the reason I was born and came into the world is to testify to the truth. Everyone on the side of truth listens to me."
>
> "What is truth?" retorted Pilate.
>
> —JOHN 18:37–38

Jesus came as the truth and to testify to the truth—the first, final, and present truth.

Judgment starts with the people of God, those who are called by His name (1 Peter 4:17).

The conditions reflect the people of God, and the remedy is through the people of God, who are called by His name (2 Chronicles 7:13–14).

The truth of the conditions of the people of God, those made in His image, is found in Hosea 4.

Hear the word of the LORD, you Israelites, because the LORD has a charge to bring against you who live in the land: "There is no faithfulness, no love, no acknowledgment of God in the land. There is only cursing, lying and murder, stealing and adultery; they break all bounds, and bloodshed follows bloodshed. Because of this the land dries up, and all who live in it waste away; the beasts of the field, the birds in the sky and the fish in the sea are swept away.

"But let no one bring a charge, let no one accuse another, for your people are like those who bring charges against a priest. You stumble day and night, and the prophets stumble with you. So I will destroy your mother—my people are destroyed from lack of knowledge.

"Because you have rejected knowledge, I also reject you as my priests; because you have ignored the law of your God, I also will ignore your children. The more priests there were, the more they sinned against me; they exchanged their glorious God for something disgraceful. They feed on the sins of my people and relish their wickedness. And it will be: Like people, like priests. I will punish both of them for their ways and repay them for their deeds.

"They will eat but not have enough; they will engage in prostitution but not flourish, because they have deserted the LORD to give themselves to prostitution; old wine and new wine take away their understanding. My people consult a wooden idol, and a diviner's rod speaks to them. A spirit of prostitution leads them astray; they are unfaithful to their God. They sacrifice on the mountaintops and burn offerings on the hills, under oak, poplar and terebinth, where the shade is pleasant. Therefore your daughters turn to prostitution and your daughters-in-law to adultery.

"I will not punish your daughters when they turn to prostitution, nor your daughters-in-law when they commit adultery, because the men themselves consort with harlots and sacrifice with shrine prostitutes—a people without understanding will come to ruin! Though you, Israel, commit adultery, do not let Judah become guilty. Do not go to Gilgal; do not go up to Beth Aven. And do not swear, 'As surely as the LORD lives!' The Israelites are stubborn, like a stubborn heifer. How then can the LORD pasture them like lambs in a meadow? Ephraim is joined to idols; leave him alone! Even when their drinks are gone, they continue their prostitution; their rulers dearly love shameful ways. A whirlwind will sweep them away, and their sacrifices will bring them shame."

The solution for the people of God, who are made in His image, is found in Isaiah 58:

"Shout it aloud, do not hold back. Raise your voice like a trumpet. Declare to my people their rebellion and to the descendants of Jacob their sins. For day after day they seek me out; they seem eager to know my ways, as if they were a nation that does what is right and has not forsaken the commands of its God. They ask me for just decisions and seem eager for God to come near them. 'Why have we fasted,' they say, 'and you have not seen it? Why have we humbled ourselves, and you have not noticed?'

"Yet on the day of your fasting, you do as you please and exploit all your workers. Your fasting ends in quarreling and strife, and in striking each other with wicked fists. You cannot fast as you do today and expect your voice to be heard on high. Is this the kind of fast I have chosen, only a day for people to humble themselves? Is it only for bowing one's head like a reed and for lying in sackcloth and ashes? Is that what you call a fast, a day acceptable to the LORD?

"Is not this the kind of fasting I have chosen: to loose the chains of injustice and untie the cords of the yoke, to set the oppressed free and break every yoke? Is it not to share your food with the hungry and to provide the poor wanderer with shelter—when you see the naked, to clothe them, and not to turn away from your own flesh and blood? Then your light will break forth like the dawn, and your healing will quickly appear; then your righteousness will go before you, and the glory of the Lord will be your rear guard. Then you will call, and the Lord will answer; you will cry for help, and he will say: Here am I. If you do away with the yoke of oppression, with the pointing finger and malicious talk, and if you spend yourselves in behalf of the hungry and satisfy the needs of the oppressed, then your light will rise in the darkness, and your night will become like the noonday.

"The Lord will guide you always; he will satisfy your needs in a sun-scorched land and will strengthen your frame. You will be like a well-watered garden, like a spring whose waters never fail. Your people will rebuild the ancient ruins and will raise up the age-old foundations; you will be called Repairer of Broken Walls, Restorer of Streets with Dwellings. If you keep your feet from breaking the Sabbath and from doing as you please on my holy day, if you call the Sabbath a delight and the Lord's holy day honorable, and if you honor it by not going your own way and not doing as you please or speaking idle words, then you will find your joy in the Lord, and I will cause you to ride in triumph on the heights of the land and to feast on the inheritance of your father Jacob." For the mouth of the Lord has spoken.

A FINAL WORD

THE WORLD IS in hot pursuit of AI: artificial intelligence.

In our day, the beginning of all things is called progressive thinking. Conversations are welcomed when discussing evolution as evidence that mankind is moving forward and becoming better than we were in the past. Our pursuits point to our end—the end we all seem to tirelessly pursue. The common aim is to end our control by recognizing that we are flawed.

Realizing that mankind falls short of what is best, our society has resolved that we must continue to evolve. The pursuit of perfection is artificial intelligence (AI), our utopia, or nirvana. AI is intended to be the highest achievement of man. If attained, it will be the pinnacle of our purpose and pursuit, the end goal of our existence. Realizing we are flawed, we seek to create fixes that would result in a better world. This better world cannot be man-made because our flaws and deficiencies are undeniable.

We hope for a better world—a better experience—and mankind is constantly working toward this perfect world and experience. AI is intended to be our answer.

There was an original solution; however, it was considered dumb and rejected by some, ignored by others, and intentionally forgotten by others still. At one time perfection was attainable.

In the beginning, perfection was given as an option to mankind, but perfection was rejected, just as it is now. Back then, man chose the option that would reflect the work of his own hands.

We, mankind, did not accept an outside remedy for our condition; we elected to take matters into our own hands. This taking matters into our own hands is AI, artificial intelligence!

We, mankind, will fix or try to fix what we know is broken. We think that because we have rejected something, it is broken, but some things do not need to be fixed because they are not broken.

We have rejected God, as we do whatever we think is right in our own eyes. With that mindset, we build things with our own hands. We call building things made in our own image progress, but by not acknowledging God, we build with artificial intelligence. We call it evolution and perfection, but it is AI—artificial intelligence.

Some people will admit it, but others will dismiss the definition of *artificial* as being false, fake, mock, unnatural, or simulated. Most people give no thought to the oxymoron *artificial intelligence.*

Man's pursuit of utopia, nirvana, or the greatest evolution is nothing new. At the beginning of all things, long before our so-called evolution, AI would have been defined as adultery and idolatry.

Perhaps our ill-fated journey and misguided pursuits are a result of what we deny or reject today that was presented in the beginning and caused our fall—the desire to be like God, knowing good and evil. Despite our inadequacies, we pursue the idea of being God. We think, "If I cannot be God, then I will use my intelligence to create God with AI." Not real but artificial intelligence. Any god created by man is not God. And anything man creates with his hands, little god as it may be, is artificial intelligence.

As we try to untangle the riddle, the conundrum, to avoid being bamboozled, there is a question rarely asked. If the question were asked and answered honestly, we would cease our man-made pursuit of perfection. That question is, How can that which has been created surpass the One who created it? Said another way, Is it possible to create something greater than ourselves? Indulgence would say, "Yes." But a thinking mind would ask, "Who created you? How can something be created that surpasses the abilities of the one who created it?" So what's the answer? We might say, "We have evolved and are now so good that we can create something that exceeds our abilities."

Just as it is impossible for reproduction between members of the same sex, so it is impossible for the created to surpass its creator.

Well, maybe not. Let's consider the idea that the created can surpass the creator. If this is possible, what is created by the creator will one day also create, and what it creates will one day be surpassed by what it created. Evolution is artificial intelligence indeed!

Evolution implies that there is no Creator because we are all creators, and there is no created, as we all are creators. It says we have arrived; we are God—not gods, but we all are God!

Abandoning the foolishness, let us get back to reason and address AI.

Tagging their pursuit as evolution, mankind seeks to progress by creating something bigger than themselves. With this pursuit, the desired outcome is that the creation surpasses its creator, and the creator serves the created.

Such a hypothesis is unreasonable and frankly ridiculous. It is without question and not for debate that we, the created—the creation, could not surpass our Creator.

We may have theories about how we can create a world in which we serve what is created, but that can never occur. There may come a day when AI serves mankind, but the machines will need man to keep them running and ready to serve.

A thinking person says, "One day, we will create machines that will serve the machines, and there will be no need for man." While there may be no need for men, there will always be a need for women!

No matter how we pursue progress, evolution will always require a Creator. AI is flawed when seen through man's eyes but pure when seen through God's eyes.

Mankind seeks a utopia and uses AI to serve himself. God says AI is the problem that leads to adultery and idolatry.

The supreme end of AI regards self. AI's goal is to reveal our misguided goals and sense of self, as well as adultery and idolatry.

Evolution is necessary for change to take place. Simply existing requires no change. God is the same—meaning He does not change and does not need to evolve. He is and shall always be…I Am.

We seek to develop or create machines that can do what we cannot. We ultimately will let go, take our hands off the wheel, abandon our control, and let our creation lead the way. Yet our continued pursuit of and insistence upon creating something beyond ourselves has, in reality, been rightly called adultery and idolatry.

BOOK CLUB DISCUSSION QUESTIONS

1. How do you define success?

2. What qualities or characteristics do you look for in a successful person?

3. What is something in your life that you held on to that you should have let go?

4. What did you learn from that experience?

5. Have you ever looked in the mirror and wondered if what you're seeing is real?

6. What are some of the common dangers associated with progress, change, or human advancement?

7. In what ways has individual choice caused confusion or division?

8. How can individual choice be destructive to a society?

9. Is there such a thing as absolute truth? Why or why not?

10. What is the source of truth?

11. Why are limits necessary in a civil society?

12. Which is more problematic, having limits or not having limits?

13. What is justice?

14. How has putting labels on ethnic groups led to injustice?

15. Is the Golden Rule still relevant in today's world? Why or why not?

16. Why is the Golden Rule no longer golden?

17. Why is it always about the money? What is "it" here? Why are relationship problems in the family and workplace often about the money?

18. Give an example of when you have been deceived by money.

19. If you had great wealth, how would you feel about the government redistributing your wealth to others?

20. Should those with great wealth be expected to share their wealth with the *have-nots*?

21. If you are a *have-not*, what one thing would you ask of someone with great wealth?

22. How has COVID changed the way you see the world?

23. How has COVID changed the way you view the role of government?

24. What do you see as lasting benefits of COVID in our families, schools, and workplaces?

25. What is society doing to reduce or eliminate poverty? What else could it do? What can you do to get involved?

26. What is society doing to reduce or eliminate ethnic tension? What else could it do? How can you participate in a solution?

INDEX

Section 6   SELF-SABOTAGE

Section 7   SOCIAL JUSTICE

Section 8   ROOTS OF DIVISION

END NOTES

Introduction

1. Matthew 5:13.

4—Sense Meets "Know Sense"

1. Proverbs 20:15.
2. Genesis 4:1, KJV
3. Genesis 3:5.
4. Genesis 3:21.
5. Revelation 3:17.

8—There Is Nothing to Lose

1. See Mark 8:36.

9—The Rules of Economics, Part 1

1. Mod Titan, "The Outer Limits Intro," YouTube, November 19, 2008, https://www.youtube.com/watch?v=8CtjhWhw2I8.

10—The Rules of Economics, Part 2

1. Mod Titan, "The Outer Limits Intro."

13—Save Me From Me

1. See 2 Timothy 3:7 and Matthew 13:15.

16—Image Is Everything

1. TheBlindSpot, "When Everyone's Super..." YouTube, December 28, 2010, https://www.youtube.com/watch?v=GYmHYQPaHaw.

17—What We've Got Here...

1. Guilherme Barbosa, "Cool Hand Luke (1967) - The Captain's speech 'What we've got here is failure to communicate,'" YouTube, August 27, 2013, https://www.youtube.com/ watch?v=452XjnaHr1A.

19—The Quest for Peace: Peace of Mind

1. See Proverbs 17:1.
2. Proverbs 13:8

20—The Quest for Peace: The Piece Ignored

1. See Luke 12:48.

21—The Quest for Peace: Picture Not Perfect Perfected

1. See Proverbs 13:22.

23—Mirror-Mirror (Reflecting All)

1. Matthew 6:22–23.
2. See Matthew 7:3–5.

24—You Got Me Going in Circles (There Are No Points in a Circle)

1. 1 Samuel 16:7.
2. Matthew 15:11.

28—The True Up

1. Dictionary.com, s.v. "true," accessed March 19, 2022, https:// www.dictionary.com/browse/trued.

31—You Scare Me!

1. Matthew 26:11.

2. Acts 20:35.

33—What's the Matter?

1. See Proverbs 22:28 and 23:10.

35—Plumb Line

1. Dictionary.com, s.v. "or," accessed March 16, 2022, https://www. dictionary.com/browse/ors.

38—Not Another Truth but the Proven Truth

1. John 8:32.

44—The Naked Truth

1. Wikipedia, s.v. "The Emperor's New Clothes," accessed April 23, 2021, https://en.wikipedia.org/wiki/The_ Emperor%27s_New_ Clothes#Plot.
2. 2 Timothy 3:6–7.

45—Nothing Is Impossible

1. See Matthew 19:24–26.

47—It Is True, Says the Lie

1. See Hebrews 11:25.

49—The Anti-Dilemma

1. Oxford Languages, s.v. "dilemma," accessed November 11, 2022, https://www.google.com/search?q=dilemma+defini tion&oq=dile mma&aqs=chrome.2.0i271j46i433i512j0i433 i512l3j0i512l4j46i433 i512.4827j0j15&sourceid=chrome&ie =UTF-8.

67–Power and Responsibility

1. "Servant Leadership Video: Martin Luther King Jr.," Leadership Geeks, accessed April 11, 2022, https://www. leadershipgeeks. com/servant-leadership-video/.

71–Voter Fraud

1. Jeremiah 17:9–10.
2. "Top 10 Unfortunate Political One-Liners," Time, accessed February 5, 2023, https://content.time.com/time/specials/ packages/article/0,28804,1859513_1859526_1859515,00. html.
3. "Top 10 Unfortunate Political One-Liners."
4. "Top 10 Unfortunate Political One-Liners."
5. Olivia Waxman, "Bill Clinton Said He 'Didn't Inhale' 25 Years Ago—But the History of U.S. Presidents and Drugs Is Much Older," Time, March 29, 2017, https:// time.com/4711887/bill-clinton-didnt-inhale-marijuana- anniversary/.

76–The Golden Rule

1. Haggai 2:6–9.

83–The Cost of Peace

1. Proverbs 17:1.
2. Proverbs 14:30.

87–Curing the Disease of Dis-Ease

1. Matthew 26:11.

92–New Wine

1. Michael Bryan, "Bible Facts: Quick Facts," Facts.net, April 10, 2020, https://facts.net/history/religion/bible-facts.

2. "Best-Selling Book," Guinness World Records
   Limited, accessed February 19, 2021, https://www.
   guinnessworldrecords.com/ world-records/best-selling-
   book-of-non-fiction.

100–Buzzer Alerts Wrong

1. 1 John 4:20.

105–Differences? There Is Only One!

1. See Romans 10:13.
2. See John 4:22.
3. See Matthew 10:6 and Matthew 15:24.
4. See Matthew 4:24; Matthew 8:16; Matthew 12:15; Luke
   4:40; Luke 5:15.
5. See John 8:44.
6. John 10:16.
7. Genesis 1:26, emphasis added.

108–Righting the Right

1. See Genesis 18:16–20 and Exodus 12:40–41.

111–As It Is in Heaven but Not on Earth

1. James 1:17, NKJV

113–The Time Is Now

1. Proverbs 9:10, KJV

117–The Best Bet

1. Acts 4:12.

About the Author

GLENN HENDERSON

Glenn Henderson is a distinguished entrepreneur and philanthropist, renowned for his remarkable achievements in the transportation and logistics industry.

He has a passion for discerning truth in a complicated world. He works with businesses to take a fresh look at best business practices, focusing on principles over lessons. He carries his message through his writings, published books, blogs, and podcasts, and by speaking to businesses, various organizations, colleges and universities, and religious groups nationally and globally.

Henderson is the founder and former CEO of AFC Worldwide, a successful global logistics transportation company. He played a pivotal role in the 9/11 relief efforts, earning national recognition for AFC's outstanding contributions. Throughout its twenty-year history, AFC Worldwide consistently set industry standards and was named Hallmark's Vendor of the Year for three consecutive years.

A serial entrepreneur, Henderson has spearheaded several businesses, including Business Accelerators and AFCLS, a logistics company. He is also the cofounder of Upscale Personal Care Home, providing care to the elderly in Jacksonville, Florida.

He has served on various boards of trustees, including Stetson University's, and currently serves on the Easterseals national board of directors.

Beyond his entrepreneurial prowess, Henderson is a recognized author of two published books. He has also developed and taught curriculum on business development/best practices at many universities, including Harvard Business School, Georgia Tech, Kennesaw State University, Stetson University, Northwestern University's Kellogg School of Management, and Beulah Heights University. This has also led him to speak at many of these prestigious academic institutions. His dedication to diversity and community service earned him the *Jacksonville Business Journal*'s Diversity Award in 2014.

Henderson and his wife live in Jacksonville, Florida. In 2014, *Ebony* magazine named the couple and their three children one of the coolest Black families in America.

**To learn more about Glenn Henderson and how you can schedule
a media interview or bring him to speak
at your company, organization, or business school,
go to www.GlennHenderson.com.**